STORYTELLING FOR STARTUPS

HOW FAST-GROWING COMPANIES CAN EMBRACE THE POWER OF STORY-DRIVEN MARKETING

MARK EVANS

Toronto, Ontario

No part of this book may be used or reproduced in any manner whatsoever with the prior written permission of the publisher, except in the case of brief quotations embodied in reviews.

This book can be purchased for educational, business or sales promotional use through Mark Evans.

This book is presented solely for educational and motivational purposes. Although the author and publisher have made every effort to ensure that the information in this book was correct at press time, the author and publisher do not assume and hereby disclaim any liability to any party for any loss, damage, or disruption caused by errors or omissions, whether such errors or omissions result from negligence, accident, or any other cause.

Library and Archives Canada Cataloguing in Publication

Evans, Mark, 1963-, author

Storytelling for startups : how fast-growing companies can embrace the power of story-driven marketing / Mark Evans.

Includes bibliographical references.

Issued in print and electronic formats.

ISBN 978-0-9940473-0-4 (pbk.).--ISBN 978-0-9940473-1-1 (pdf)

1. Marketing. 2. Branding (Marketing). 3. Advertising. I. Title.

HF5415.E94 2015   658.8   C2015-901301-1

C2015-901302-X

Text copyright © 2015 Mark Evans markevans.ca

Cover and Book Design: 2015 © Doris Chung Publisher Production Solutions www.publisher-ps.com www.selfpublishing.today

Cover illustrations and chapter illustrations: 2015 © Kevin Sylvester www.kevinsylvesterbooks.com

ISBN (print): 978-0-9940473-0-4 | (ePub): 978-0-9940473-1-1

Printed in Canada

To my wife, Pamela, for her enthusiasm, support and love – none of this would have been possible without you. To my children, Isabel, Julia and Elias, for keeping me grounded, motivated and in the moment. To my parents and family for always being there.

TABLE OF CONTENTS

Forward vi
Acknowledgements vii
Introduction – Storytelling in a time-strapped, multi-tasking world.. 1

Part I – The Art of Storytelling...and how it drives business success

Chapter 1 - The Keys to Great Storytelling 9
Chapter 2 - Why Steve Jobs was a Great Storyteller 19
Chapter 3 - Time for Startups to Embrace Storytelling 27
Chapter 4 - What's Your Story, Morning Glory? 35
Chapter 5 - Diving into the Messaging Process.......................... 41
Chapter 6 - Messaging Deliverables 61

Part II – Your Storytelling Audiences...and where to find them

Chapter 7 - Discovering The Audience For Your Stories 75
Chapter 8 - Talking to Your Customers 91
Chapter 9 - Creating a Storytelling/Marketing Strategy 99
Chapter 10 - Defining and Measuring Storytelling Success....111

Part III – Who Gets to Tell Stories?

Chapter 11 - Who Gets To Tell Stories?.. 121
Chapter 12 - Influencers Are Storytellers Too 129
Chapter 13 - Setting the Stage for Media Coverage................. 139

Part IV- Attracting the Spotlight…and how to keep it

Chapter 14 - The Secret Formula For Attracting Media Coverage 151
Chapter 15 - Picking the Time and Place for PR 161
Chapter 16 - How to Keep the Storytelling Machine Going.... 173

Part V- Okay, Let's Tell Some Stories

Chapter 17 - Tell, Don't Sell 179
Chapter 18 - An Insider's Take on Storytelling 187
Chapter 19 - The Building Blocks for Websites That Work...... 189
Chapter 20 - Celebrating Your Customers' Success 201
Chapter 21 - Using Videos to Pack a Punch............................... 209
Chapter 22 - Leveraging Social Media to Engage 217
Chapter 23 - Jump-Start Your Marketing With Blogging.......... 223
Chapter 24 - Tapping Into the Popularity of Infographics 231
Chapter 25 - Creating White Papers That Have Sizzle.............. 237
Chapter 26 - Email Newsletters that Get Read......................... 243
Chapter 27 - The Press Release is Alive and Well 249
Chapter 28 - Going Against the Grain with Podcasting........... 255
Chapter 29 - Telling Stories to Live Audiences 259
Conclusion - The Time for Storytelling is Now 263
Reading List 266
Notes 267

FOREWARD

First, let's talk about that word "story."

"Story" and "storytelling" are two of those words that I sometimes find impossibly squishy in a business context. For me, they often conjure up more performance art than business.

But here's the thing: The idea of storytelling as it applies to business isn't about spinning a yarn or fairytale.

Rather, it's about how your business (or its products or services) exist in the real world: who you are and what you do for others – how you add value to people's lives, ease their troubles, help shoulder their burdens, and meet their needs.

At its heart, a compelling brand story is a gift that gives your audience a way to connect with you as one person to another, and to view your business as what it is: a living, breathing entity run by real people offering real value.

In that way, your content is not about "storytelling", it's about telling a true story well.

So how do you pull compelling stories out of your own organization? How do you tell your own brand story in a way that relates to your customer?

That's the question at the heart of the book you're now holding in your hands.

Let's do this.

Ann Handley
Author of the Wall Street Journal best-seller, *Everybody Writes:*
Your Go-To Guide to Creating Ridiculously Good Content **(Wiley)**
www.annhandley.com

ACKNOWLEDGEMENTS

Thanks to the following people for their support and participation in helping in the creation of this book:

Marcus Sheridan
Ann Handley
Ben Plomion
Christina O'Reilly
Jay Baer
Melissa Shapiro
Randy Frisch
Mark Hardy
Stuart MacDonald
Shawn Arora
Neil Bhapkar
Lee Odden
Rebecca Reeves
Chikodi Chima
Cezary Pietrzak
Peter J. Thomson
Simon Sinek
Marty Neumeier
Lee LeFever
Jamie Schulman
Robleh Jama
Frank Falcone
Summer Liu
Michael Katchen
Mike McDerment
Renee Warren
Evgeny Tchebotarev
Michael Grieve
Viktoria Kjkrstic

Kerry Liu
Ben Baldwin
Mitch Joel
Leesa Renee Hall
Bryan McCaw
Peep Laja
Lior Degani
Peter Pietrzkiewicz
Kevin Sylvester
Kelly Norgate
Jeff Goldenberg
Sean Evans
Brian Teeney
Mitch Solway
HubSpot
Punk Ave
Crazy Egg
Moz
Pipedrive
Pocket
Mailchimp
Balsamiq
Tap Influence
Wistia
The Gorge
RateHub
Doris Chung
Leigh Fowler

INTRODUCTION

The children's television host Mr. Rogers always carried in his wallet a quote from a social worker that said, "Frankly, there isn't anyone you couldn't learn to love once you've heard their story." And the way I like to interpret that is probably the greatest story commandment, which is "Make me care" -- please, emotionally, intellectually, aesthetically, just make me care.
  - **Andrew Stanton**

In my professional career, stories have played a leading role. As a newspaper reporter, entrepreneur and startup marketing consultant, I always believed that while content is king, stories are the shining stars. Having easily attained Malcolm Gladwell's "10,000 hours" rule when it comes to storytelling, I'm convinced there is a new and captivating approach to doing business: story-driven marketing.

What is story-driven marketing?

It is a way of immersing people in your brand and products by appealing to their emotions and interests as much as their needs. Let's be abundantly clear: it is about marketing and selling but also delivering insight and information by engaging, educating and entertaining target audiences - not by bombarding or patronizing them. It is about stories that create immersive and authentic experiences, as opposed to the "me, me, me" marketing approach that companies use to talk about their products and the features that supposedly impress customers, partners and investors.

Story-driven marketing is powerful for a simple reason: everyone likes - actually, loves - a good story. It is an integral part of who we are as humans. We like to tell and share stories. We remember stories, not facts and statistics. As literary scholar and author Jonathan Gottschall says, "Stories are the fabric of our social lives". Telling stories is how information is effectively and creatively packaged and shared. As children, we learn to love stories. Stories are how children (including my three children) learn to relate to others and the world around them. Stories encourage them to develop empathy, curiosity, passions and vivid imaginations, and embrace new ideas. When children hear a story, it is easy for them to become part of the story as opposed to simply listening. This is powerful and magical. And as we grow up, our love for stories does not disappear; the stories just change their shape and form. From a scientific perspective, stories work because our brains are hardwired for them. The limbic system processes emotions in the same part of the brain that makes decisions.

Why does story-driven marketing work?

Story-driven marketing works because it is a natural way to communicate. It is not broadcasting (aka traditional marketing), but real and appealing stories that pull people into your world, brand and products. For example, think about the emotional power of Budweiser's television commercials featuring the bond between a puppy and a Clydesdale (http://bit.ly/1JeAYRu). While the commercials do not feature beer, they draw people into the brand with stories that drive strong connections.

In the last 20 years, the marketing world has seen momentous changes. Brands can no longer saturate the market with advertising to raise awareness and drive sales. With more information than ever at their fingertips, consumers have little interest in the type of marketing in which a company rambles on and on about features and prices. Consumers already have that information, so they are looking for something different and something better.

The biggest marketing challenge today is getting time-strapped, information-overloaded consumers to pay attention. To get them engaged, brands need to establish a personal connection. Stories are *the* way to make this happen. Smart brands have no choice but to embrace story-driven marketing as the foundation for how they do business.

What does story-driven marketing involve?

It is a better way to do marketing but it requires companies to behave differently. More importantly, story-driven marketing requires companies to abandon many of their traditional approaches and tools. The emergence of story-driven marketing reflects the changing marketing and sales landscape, which has forced companies to discover new ways to connect with consumers. In particular, the new marketing landscape has seen the rapid rise of social media and content marketing. Social media is a way to share content with a global audience and have "conversations", but I would argue there are shortcomings when it comes to using Facebook, Twitter and Pinterest, et al as storytelling vehicles. Forrester Research analyst Nate

Elliot, for example, says Twitter and Facebook are ineffective for many brands due to low reach and engagement, which is the opposite of story-driven marketing.

Meanwhile, content marketing has become all the rage as brands are told they need to create content (blogs, case studies, videos, e-books, tutorials, etc.) so they can win over customers with something that is not seen as blatant advertising. But content marketing - at least the way many brands are doing it - is corporate marketing and sales collateral in shiny, user-friendly packaging (aka a wolf in sheep's clothing).

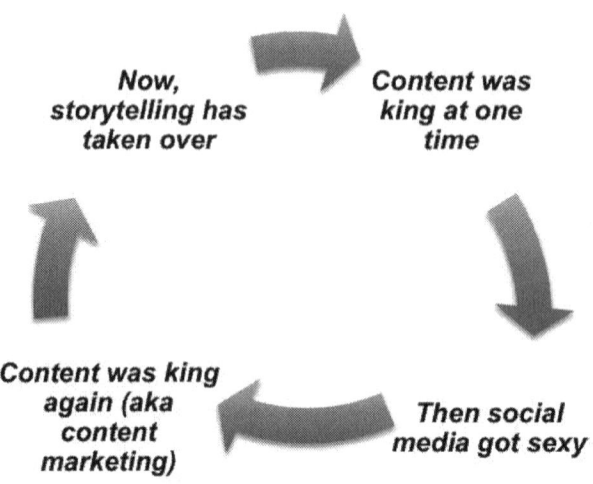

Story-driven marketing and this book

Fortunately, there is a better way: story-driven marketing. To provide strategic and tactical insight into how to embrace and capitalize on story-driven marketing, this book is divided into five sections:

1. The history, benefits and keys to storytelling, including a focus on some of the best storytelling entrepreneurs.

2. Creating a "core" story that articulates what your startup does and the value it delivers to customers.

3. Discovering the audiences for your stories, identifying and talking to customers, and creating a storytelling strategy.

4. Deciding who should tell your stories – internal and external storytellers – and how to prepare and train them.

5. Guidance, best practices and tactical steps to create stories using a variety of formats.

This book will help you embrace the concept of story-driven marketing to make your company's marketing and sales efforts more compelling and successful. Equally important, it will drive deeper relationships with your customers. The book features case studies that highlight story-driven marketing in action. As much as I can talk about the value of story-driven marketing, real-world stories make ideas and concepts come to life.

While most people understand the appeal of stories, I can see how there could be questions about story-driven marketing. You may ask, "How can stories drive my business, and how do I create stories? Don't I need creative people to make it happen?" These questions are understandable because story-driven marketing is a new concept that can take time to appreciate, comprehend and embrace. That said, I believe the barriers to entry are low because most people inherently understand the impact, power and influence of stories. And, as important, everyone can be creative; it is just a matter of unlocking their creativity and allowing it to flourish.

Who should read this book?

This book is designed for entrepreneurs and, for that matter, people who want to grow their businesses and who believe storytelling can play a key role in their success. They recognize stories can give their startup a competitive edge, create an exciting brand personality, and, in the process, drive higher sales. With a commitment to storytelling, this book will give you the option to explore two paths.

1. With insight into best practices and tactics, entrepreneurs can develop their own stories. You may not be the best storyteller out of the gate, but you will have enough knowledge and confidence to head in the right direction. You will begin a storytelling journey that will lead you in different, unexpected and fascinating directions. One of the best things about storytelling is not knowing the path it will take. This makes storytelling compelling, interesting and, often, surprising and memorable.

2. If the do-it-yourself approach is a non-starter, this book will provide the guidance to understand how storytelling can help your startup succeed. This book will improve your ability to find the right people to create your stories and the kind of stories to tell. No more stabs in the dark, or being sold a bill of goods by marketers selling "snake oil". Think of this book as a "cheat sheet" for storytelling so you can the hire the right people to lead projects with confidence.

Whether you subscribe to option one or option two, it is about smart entrepreneurs ready to capitalize on the power of storytelling to seize new opportunities and competitive openings.

How to use this book

In reading this book, entrepreneurs should begin to see storytelling as not only a necessity but also something they can embrace to be more successful - be it higher sales and leads, more engaged customers and employees, or brands with a distinct personality. Each section will give you first-hand insight into how entrepreneurs and startups embraced storytelling. At the end of each chapter, there is a key takeaway, a list of questions to help you get started and, as important, spark ideas and conversations, and an exercise to embrace a key concept. There are different ways to use this book. It may be something you read once. It may be something that you bookmark and keep on your desk.

Story-driven marketing is how your business will stand apart and thrive at a time when the world is becoming increasingly noisy with companies aggressively using online advertising, content marketing and social media to super-charge their marketing and sales efforts. Companies that want to dominate their markets or, at the very least, be vibrant players need to tell good stories because it is the way to connect and build relationships with consumers and outflank rivals.

The time for story-driven marketing is now.

CHAPTER ONE
The Keys to Great Storytelling

"Storytelling is, by far, the most under-rated skill in business"
- Gary Vaynerchuk, serial entrepreneur, author and startup investor

Storytelling is more important than ever.

Companies that tell great stories, win. Companies that don't, lose.

In today's digital age, people are busy and multi-tasking. They are distracted and overwhelmed by a tsunami of information. According to a report done by the University of California (San Diego), the average person sees and hears more than 100,000 words per day of content - TV, radio, social media, video games, text messages and the Internet. Given how much information people are consuming, it is becoming more difficult for brands to capture their attention, even for a short period of time.

For companies of all shapes and sizes, this has created huge challenges and opportunities. While there are more tools than ever to communicate with consumers, there is a massive amount of competition. When every company is aggressively trying to reach consumers using multiple channels, it is becoming more problematic to be heard above the fray. As much as companies offer valuable products or services, their efforts often go unnoticed and unrewarded because they fail to capture the interest or attention of consumers.

So what should companies do? Do they advertise more, embrace the never-ending number of social media platforms, turn themselves into content publishers, or try to shout louder than the next guy? While there are plenty of marketing options, I believe the most effective approach is straightforward: Tell stories that are immersive and engaging.

For inspiration, look no further than Chipotle Mexican Grill, the gourmet taco and burrito restaurant chain, which has embraced storytelling in truly creative and compelling ways. Its *"Scarecrow"* video (http://bit.ly/1wqByVe) is wonderful storytelling – dramatic, gripping, imaginative, intriguing and inspiring. The story works because it reflects Chipotle's brand values – "food with integrity". To drive home the story, Chipotle also created a video game that infuses education and entertainment into the company's brand vision.

"Chipotle is not talking about burritos or something pedestrian," says Ann Handley, a content marketing strategist. "They are talking about a bigger story - making the world a little better, not just for Chipotle but its customers too."

Storytelling is not a new idea

Storytelling has always been part of the marketing landscape. But the importance of storytelling has arguably never been higher. Today, people are distracted so it is difficult for brands to get people to listen to what they are saying. If you are not telling stories, you need to climb on the bandwagon now. Otherwise, you risk being left behind by rivals that understand that storytelling is a powerful way to establish a competitive edge.

What is storytelling?

"Storytelling is a powerful way to put ideas into the world today" – Robert McKee, creative writing and screenwriting instructor

Everyone likes good stories. Stories are memorable, powerful, magical, authentic, emotional, inspiring, educational and entertaining. They can spark conversations, dialogue and community building. Stories let you share different ideas in ways that are easy to deliver and consume. Storytelling is about creating connections, building relationships, engaging people, and yes, making purchases. "Stories can be a way for humans to feel that we have control over the world," Cody C. Delistraty, wrote in *The Atlantic*. "They allow people to see patterns where there is chaos, meaning where there is randomness. Humans are inclined to see narratives where there are none because it can afford meaning to our lives - a form of existential problem solving."

As humans, we have always been storytellers. The history of storytelling goes back to prehistoric men who told stories by drawing on the walls of caves. In ancient Greece, people such as Homer told stories through poems. As books started to be produced in the fifth century, storytelling became more formal. The invention of Johannes Gutenberg's printing press in 1436 helped to push storytelling into the mainstream. In the 20th century, storytelling reached mass audiences with the invention and proliferation of radio, movies and television.

Today, everyone can be a storyteller through the Web, social media and content marketing. As a result, the storytelling landscape has been democratized because everyone has a global distribution platform for words, images and video (aka the Internet). With so many storytelling services (e.g. YouTube, Facebook, blogs, Twitter, Pinterest, Instagram, etc.), the barriers to good storytelling are commitment and creativity. It is important to realize storytelling is a fluid, dynamic process. You are drawing a line in the sand rather than etching something in stone. Stories need to constantly evolve and change. Sometimes, a story has to be updated because a company has expanded or moved in a different direction. In other cases, a story may have to be refreshed because the competitive landscape has shifted. There could be a new rival with a sexy, exciting story capturing the spotlight. (Note: Think about how Blackberry's story failed to change when the iPhone appeared). Recapturing the spotlight could require a new and/or great story to be quickly created.

What makes for a good story?

At the end of the day, good stories achieve three things: they engage, educate and entertain. So what do we mean by engage, educate and entertain?

One of the biggest challenges facing startups is getting people to pay attention to what they are doing and selling. Startups not only want people to be interested, they want to spark curiosity, excitement and, hopefully, an action - a sale, download, registration, etc. By engaging them, people will talk about your products online and off-line. That's powerful.

Education is also a big storytelling goal for startups. When people are interested in a product, the sales cycle takes a big leap forward. You can educate them about what your product does, the benefits and features. Education is particularly important when doing business in an emerging market or offering a new way to do things. For example, I attended a conference in the early 1990s in which Amazon.com's Jeff Bezos explained that books could now be bought on the Web - a radical concept at the time.

To see some great examples of educational storytelling, check out Common Craft's video library - http://www.commoncraft.com/videolist. One of Common Craft's earliest and most popular videos is *"Twitter in Plain English"* (http://bit.ly/1ys5d0R). When you watch the video today, it seems simplistic but, at the time, Twitter was a small social media platform, although it was teeming with enthusiastic users. The video did an excellent job of explaining how Twitter worked and how people would use it.

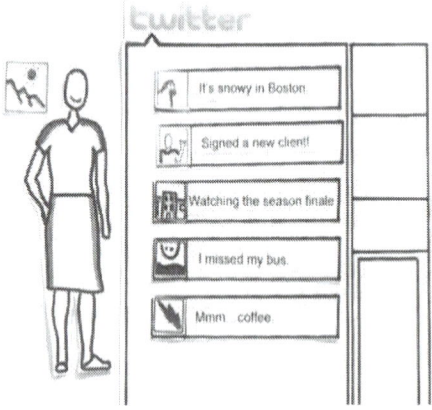

But what about entertain? Why should startup storytelling be entertaining? Let's face it, not every story has to be formal and business-like. Sometimes, it makes sense to go against the grain or think out of the box. Using stories to entertain people can be an effective way to communicate information in a fun way. Startups should not be afraid to entertain because it can build a distinct brand personality.

What are keys to good storytelling?

Story-driven marketing comes down to a few key ingredients.

1. Being customer-centric: Many startups fail at storytelling because they talk about themselves and their products. Frankly, customers do not care about what you do or your technology. They care about what your product does for them. Marcus Sheridan, a content marketing consultant, says storytelling needs a purpose. "There is a bad way and good way to tell stories. Consumers care about themselves, so unless the story resonates with me and I can see me in a story, it is not very valuable".

A great example of a customer-centric startup is Zappos, the popular online shoe retailer. Zappos created an army of loyal customers by accepting returns with no questions asked, sending flowers to customers, and even providing a late-night caller with information on where to order a pizza.

2. Commitment: Good storytelling happens by doing it repeatedly. Some stories flow easily, while some require work – practice, rewrites and new approaches. Success occurs when startups invest the time, resources and effort.

3. Focus: It is challenging to be all things to all people, and it is hard to tell stories everywhere. With limited resources, startups must tell stories where target audiences reside. It means focusing on a small number of storytelling opportunities.

4. **Personality:** Good stories happen when an authentic personality shines through. It is the difference between creating content, and developing stories that people find interesting, intriguing or provocative.

5. **Opportunity:** Sometimes, stories happen because there is a well-defined plan. Sometimes, good stories happen because a situation emerges that screams for action. For example, it could be breaking news or an event that a startup can leverage by spinning a related story.

During last year's World Cup, StickerYou jumped on the bandwagon by placing industrial-strength stickers that featured the flags of different countries on sidewalks around Toronto. It then successfully pitched a story to the media about how it was helping to fuel World Cup fever.

6. Courage: Yup, courage. Becoming a storyteller means stepping into the spotlight. Even with a lot of work, it is not a slam-dunk that people will like your stories or find them engaging. But success involves risk. Not every story is going to work…and that's okay.

7. A willingness to listen, not just tell: As much as you want to tell stories, listening is important. Often, ideas for stories emerge when you're listening. It could be at a conference, a dinner party or out for drinks with friends. If you are not listening, good story opportunities are squandered.

By now, you should have a better idea about the value of stories. For many companies, one of the biggest realities of marketing is the number of options. Every option involves opportunities and risks, and there is no guarantee of success as business depends on multiple variables. So how do small and large companies mitigate their marketing risk? The best option is storytelling. It is *the* way to connect with consumers, regardless of the channels used to reach them.

KEY TAKEAWAY:

Stories can connect with people in many different ways. Creating stories hinges on a willingness to jump on the proverbial bandwagon, and then keep going.

"A great storyteller...helps people figure out not only what matters in the world, but also why it matters." – Maria Popova

KEY QUESTIONS:

1. How can we embrace storytelling?

2. What makes a good story great?

3. How can stories engage, educate and entertain?

4. Who within your company is best positioned to tell stories?

5. Do we have the appetite to embrace storytelling as a long-term journey?

EXERCISE

Get together for a brainstorming session to discover startups that are good storytellers, and why they are so effective. Then, write down the different kinds of stories that your startup could create to engage, educate and entertain customers.

CHAPTER TWO

Why Steve Jobs was a Great Storyteller

"Those who tell the stories rule the world."
-Hopi American Indian proverb

There are different kinds of stories to be created and there are different kinds of storytellers. Jake Sorofman, a digital marketing analyst with Gartner Inc., an IT research and advisory company, divided brand storytellers into five categories:

1. The Evangelist, who combines stories with wisdom and practical advice to guide audiences – Robert Scoble, Guy Kawasaki, Vinton Cerf

2. The Skeptic, who takes umbrage at conventional beliefs (aka as a disrupter or shit disturber) – Steve Colbert, Ralph Nader

3. The Jester, who uses humour to tell stories but also inserts insight and wisdom into the mix – Mark Twain, Garrison Keillor, Jon Stewart.

4. The Helper, who is focused on meeting the needs of target audiences by offering insight – Walter Mossberg

5. The Visionary, who illuminates the future and how you need to start thinking to embrace it – Steve Jobs, Henry Ford, Sam Walton

When we think about the most dynamic entrepreneurs, we often refer to them as super-salesmen. These are people who get people excited about their products - even if the products are a nice-to-have rather than a need-to-have. They are people who, for a variety of reasons, can quickly establish a strong, visceral connection with potential and existing customers. They have the ability to bring people "inside the tent" in a way that is compelling and enticing. In some respects, it is almost as if they are doing you a favour by telling you about their products.

There is another way to describe these people: they are storytellers in their own way, approach and style. There are many of these storytellers, but let's put the spotlight on two of the best: Apple's Steve Jobs, who made personal computers and mobile devices cool and sexy, and Ronco's Ron Popeil, who convinced many men that the best way to deal with baldness was using spray-on hair (aka "Great Looking Hair Formula #9").

What do Jobs and Popeil share other than being entrepreneurs who enjoyed tremendous success? They had passion, relentless drive, distinctive personalities and a flair for the dramatic. Storytelling allowed them to establish a bigger than life stature and attract an enthusiastic group of believers, evangelists and happy customers.

Featureflash / Shutterstock.com

Steve Jobs as a master storyteller

Steve Jobs is revered as a product and marketing genius. His passion for perfection, love of design and fixation with the smallest details played crucial roles in the launch of the iPod, iPhone and iPad. Jobs' ability to nurture and micro-manage the development of products that delighted consumers transformed Apple from a struggling niche player into the world's best-known and most valuable brand. Jobs was also great at telling stories that captivated, enthralled, inspired and drew people into his world. When Jobs gave a presentation, the audience was completely engaged and ready to take whatever cue delivered, even when it had a good idea of what was coming.

A perfect example of Jobs' storytelling brilliance was the launch of the iPhone in 2007 at the MacWorld conference. Even though the high-tech world was buzzing with speculation that Apple was going to put a telephone inside an iPod, Jobs' keynote was an amazing storytelling performance. With the crowd already on the edge of its seat, Jobs stoked their excitement by slowly building the tension:

> *"This is a day I've been looking forward to for two and a half years. Every once in a while a revolutionary product comes along that changes everything. One is very fortunate if you get to work on just one of these in your career. Apple has been very fortunate that it's been able to introduce a few of these into the world. In 1984 we introduced the Macintosh. It didn't just change Apple, it changed the whole industry. In 2001 we introduced the first iPod, and it didn't just change the way we all listened to music, it changed the entire music industry."*

> *"Well, today, we're introducing THREE revolutionary new products. The first one is a widescreen iPod with touch controls,"* the crowd goes wild. *"The second is a revolutionary new mobile phone. And the third

is a breakthrough Internet communications device. An iPod, a phone, an Internet mobile communicator. An iPod, a phone, an Internet mobile communicator... these are NOT three separate devices! And we are calling it iPhone!"

By the time, Jobs got to, "and we are calling it iPhone!" the crowd had nearly lost their minds. The response was rapturous and wildly enthusiastic. Truth be told, the market would probably have gone bananas about the iPhone if Apple had simply issued a press release, but the launch was more successful and far more dramatic due to Jobs' expertise in telling a story. The iPhone was not only a new communications device but also a significant moment in technology history.

So what made Jobs such a powerful storyteller?

It could have been his fervent belief in Apple being more than just a company that made computing devices. Jobs saw Apple as a rebellion, a movement, and a leading anti-establishment player. And people identified with this notion of rebellion! Look at the success of the Apple (hipster) vs. PC (nerd) commercials featuring Justin Long and John Hodgman. Apple's brand persona, in many ways, reflected Jobs' personal experiences and beliefs. As Apple's CEO and spiritual leader, Jobs had a knack for convincing people they were part of something bigger, better and different. Without coming across as a slick salesmen or preachy, Jobs leveraged narratives to drive home the Apple message to audiences willing to believe. When Jobs spoke, it was not just a CEO talking but a storyteller in action.

Ron Popeil: "But wait, there's more"

Another entrepreneur with a gift for storytelling is Ron Popeil, who pitched Ronco products for years on late-night television. Anyone who ever saw infomercials for the Showtime Rotisserie ("Set it, and forget it"), the Electric Food Dehydrator ("How easy is it?"), The Smokeless Ashtray ("For the smoker who cares about his family") or the Pocket Fisherman ("The biggest fishing invention since the hook") can appreciate Popeil's storytelling skills.

When you think about it, Popeil was selling household products that were mostly nice-to-haves, rather than need-to-haves. I mean, does anyone really need a mini-fishing rod? But Popeil had an uncanny ability to capture your attention by telling stories about each product - how they could be used, how they made your life easier, how they were better than other products....and how affordable they were. Popeil's trademark storytelling phrase was "But wait, there's more", which only increased the anticipation. The more you watched Popeil pitch, the more your interest grew. As someone who learned how to sell on the streets of Chicago in the 1950s Popeil was a natural at establishing a connection by appealing to the emotions, aspirations and needs of potential customers. "I talked, I yelled, I hawked, and it worked! I was stuffing money into my pockets, more money than I had ever seen in my life," Popeil said about how he started to sell kitchen products on Chicago's Maxwell St. "I didn't have to be poor the rest of my life. Through selling, I could escape from poverty and the miserable existence I had with my grandparents. I had lived for 16 years in homes without love, and now I finally found a form of affection and human connection through sales."

What made Popeil such a good storyteller is he understood the importance of creating tension, drama and expectation. Rather than asking someone to make a purchase right away, he would start by telling a story, talk about the product's benefits (not features), and only then ask people if they wanted to buy it. There was no doubt that Popeil was selling at all times, but he camouflaged his pitch with storytelling that took you on an emotional journey, even though you knew how things were going to end: Popeil finally disclosing the price of the product and how you could order it – usually in "four easy payments". And you know Popeil's stories resonated when his products and sales pitches became an ingrained part of pop culture.

While Jobs and Popeil are two good examples of storytelling entrepreneurs, the list could easily include people such as P.T. Barnum, Richard Branson and Tony Robbins. Yes, they are polished, persuasive and engaging speakers with a passion for entrepreneurship, but they all mastered the ability to create compelling narratives elegantly layered over sales pitches. When Branson speaks, writes or does PR stunts, he is crafting stories around his personal brand, corporate brands and products. In immersing ourselves in Branson's storytelling, we subconsciously digest his sales efforts. If you are wondering why Branson has been so successful, look no further than his ability to leverage story-driven marketing.

KEY TAKEAWAY:

Many of the world's most successful entrepreneurs are master storytellers. They have the ability to wrap marketing and sales into a compelling narrative, and deliver it to the masses.

"The storyteller sets the vision, values and agenda of an entire generation that is to come, and Disney has a monopoly on the storyteller business. You know what? I am tired of that bullshit, I am going to be the next storyteller." - Steve Jobs

KEY QUESTIONS:

1. Who are the storytellers in your organization?

2. How can you teach your employees to become better storytellers?

3. What are their strengths and weaknesses?

4. How can successful storytellers inspire you?

5. How can your company create and encourage a storytelling culture?

EXERCISE:

Think about the people in your lives who are terrific storytellers. What makes their stories so engrossing, entertaining and engaging – stories that would not have the same impact if told by someone else? Who are the "storytellers" that you would invite to a dinner party?

CHAPTER THREE:
Time for Startups to Embrace Storytelling

"People do not buy goods and services. They buy relations, stories and magic."
- Seth Godin

Creating good stories is how startups convince preoccupied consumers that there is something worth their time and interest. Whether a startup's stories engage, educate or entertain, they capture enough of the spotlight to get a consumer to pause, even if it is for a short time. If you get can someone to stop in their tracks, it is an opportunity to tell your story. Storytelling is how scrappy and hard-driving startups build relationships with customers, employees, partners, the media or investors.

But here's the key question: how do startups get started with storytelling? The answer: a four-step process that any startup can embrace.

1. The first and most important step is recognizing that every startup can be a storyteller and every startup has good stories to tell. Anyone who thinks otherwise is wrong. As humans, we tell stories all the time. We tell stories to our children, during sales presentations, in the dressing room after hockey games, during dinner parties, and at coffee meetings. Storytelling is an integral part of how every human lives and connects with other people. This includes startup entrepreneurs who need to tell stories about their company's products, employees, competitors and marketplace. It is storytelling that happens in a particular venue, but it is still storytelling.

Here is a list of 10 questions to kick off your storytelling journey:
1. What inspired you to launch your startup?
2. How difficult was it to become an entrepreneur?
3. Are you solving a problem that you encountered?
4. What have been the biggest challenges along the way?
5. What are the biggest lessons you have learned?
6. What are the mistakes you have made?
7. What are the keys to success?

8. What are your goals?
9. How do you hire people?
10. What has surprised you about being an entrepreneur?

These are straightforward questions, but people love to hear personal stories about an entrepreneur's goals, challenges and successes. Coming up with stories is like meeting someone at a party. In many cases, people have interesting stories to tell; you just have to ask them questions. In creating stories, you are answering questions, making observations about the things you are seeing and doing, and the people you are meeting.

2. Think about your target audience (aka the people who will, hopefully, be consuming your stories). What stories would *they* want to hear as opposed to the stories you want to tell them? As a storyteller, the number one task is making audiences happy, so stories have to be about them and their needs. You have to ask yourself, "Will this story be interesting to my audience?"

3. Start to collect story ideas about your product, customers, competitors and the market. Like a reporter, you are looking for stories that are new, interesting, unique, different or provocative. Not every idea will become a story, but having many ideas makes it easier for good stories to emerge. Storytelling is a state of mind and recognizing that storytelling opportunities exist everywhere.

4. "Just Do It" - aka start creating stories. It could begin with a story on your Website about how your startup was created. A story could be a blog post, a Facebook update with a link to an interesting article, or a photograph posted on social media. They do not need to be perfect stories. It is more important to build momentum so the storytelling process can be established.

The Problem: Why are startups bad storytellers?

If good stories are so important, why don't most startups tell them?

This is a multi-faceted question. The simplest answer is most startups are bad storytellers because they have little knowledge or insight about how to create stories. [Note: There is insight, best practices and case studies on how to create stories beginning in Chapter 19).

Don't get me wrong, startup entrepreneurs are smart and passionate, but I have worked with dozens of start-ups and storytelling is not a core skill I have come across. For the most part, storytelling is not something they learned or attempted to do. Frankly, it is not something they understand or see as a key part of starting and growing a company.

"In general, whether it's marketing, branding, messaging or storytelling, startups are either bad at it or not aware of the glue that holds all of it together," says Cezary Pietrzak, a marketing and mobile consultant. "When it comes to storytelling, the stories come from the founders and their vision to change the world. But after that foundation, the continuity of the story gets difficult." Translation: entrepreneurs are often lousy storytellers.

For most startups, product is king, which explains why most of their time, energy and resources are devoted to building a product. The love affair with product often means adding more features in a desperate attempt to attract more consumers. Lee LeFever, co-founder of Common Craft, which produces corporate videos, says the focus on product and features often causes startups to forget how people use their products. "You want to get people to see the beauty of using your product in the real world, and a story is a good way to do it," he said.

AN INSIDER'S TAKE ON STARTUP STORYTELLING

While many startups ideas are innovative, people can be skeptical when asked to embrace something new and different.

This is where storytelling can be extremely effective by creating a narrative that makes it easier for people to see how a new product meets their needs. You want them to see how it fits into their world, rather than have them focus on the technology.

This reality is something that Karl Martin, founder and CEO with Nymi, faces on a regular basis. Nymi makes wearable technology that uses your heart's unique signature to unlock devices, remember passwords and authenticate your identity. It is leading-edge technology that requires a big leap of faith.

Martin says storytelling allows Nymi to talk about how it is offering a better way to use passwords, payment cards and PIN numbers. This is a concept that consumers understand because it is a part of their everyday lives. "My ideas around storytelling are driven by a basic sense of empathy for the person on the other side," Martin says. "You want people to buy into your vision. The analogy is skipping a stone. You are trying to skip a stone as far as possible and have your audience come along for the ride. If you start a story by saying here is what I do but offer no context, you are taking a big rock and dropping it in the water."

For Nymi, the challenge is how to make good storytelling happen. Martin says one of the keys is creating a solid, consumer-friendly story, and then continually repeating so it seeps into the corporate culture. As important, Martin says everything that Nymi does publicly – product demos, presentations, etc. – begins with a story that provides context, rather than the technology being developing. "As a technology company, it is easy to have technology take

> over the story. Our culture is about making sure an outward-facing story has context."
>
> For entrepreneurs, Martin says it is important to realize that storytelling is about getting people to buy into something they may not do on their own. "I think startup entrepreneurs see storytelling as marketing; good marketing involves telling stories. They don't realize that storytelling is not about finding customers, but getting them to buy into the concept about why you exist as a company."

The value of corporate lore

As much as startups should focus on meeting the needs of customers, it does not mean they have to have a customer-centric approach all the time. One of the most effective ways for startups to engage target audiences is creating a narrative around their corporate history. Many people are interested in why an entrepreneur decided to create a startup. What were their motivations? What were the problems they wanted to solve? What were some of the early hurdles to overcome, or the successes they achieved? If done authentically, a company's history can create an emotional connection with customers.

> Some good examples of leveraging corporate lore include:
>
> The private materialized spark for Uber, the world's most successful car and ride-sharing service, reportedly materialized when Garrett Camp and Travis Kalanick could not find a taxi during the Le Web conference in Paris. It reminded them about how difficult it was to get a taxi in their hometown, San Francisco. Camp and Kalanick channeled their frustration into a service that addresses the pain points of many people. Today, Uber is a $40-billion company.

You may wonder how serial entrepreneur Richard Branson decides to create a new business. The launch of Virgin Airlines was sparked by a girl he was supposed to meet in, not surprisingly, the Virgin Islands. On his way to meet her, his flight to the islands was cancelled. Disappointed but determined, Branson chartered a plane, even though he could not afford it. He then walked around the airport with a blackboard that advertised flights to the island for $29, which he promptly sold to the other waiting passengers.

Mark Benioff was feeling stifled after working for Larry Ellison at Oracle. The "story" is that Benioff leaves Oracle and proclaims that software is dead and SaaS is the future. This was not a new concept; analysts had been talking about the end of software, but Benioff made the story resonate with a wide audience. Salesforce used the tagline "No Software" for years.

The Toronto-based company, located in the basement of co-founder Mike McDerment's parents' house, was running a search engine optimization business. As the story goes, McDerment could not find a good invoicing service, so Freshbooks decided to build one. Fast-forward 12 years; Freshbooks has more than five million customers. McDerment said corporate history is important because it provides people with context about where the company came from and where it is going.

KEY TAKEAWAY:

Storytelling is an absolute necessity for startups looking for an edge in an ultra-competitive world. Startups that are good storytellers can better engage and connect with target audiences - customers, employees, partners, media and investors.

"Figuring out what story you want to tell is tricky. It is thinking less about storytelling, and telling true stories well - an original story, a real story that is different than competitors." - Ann Handley

KEY QUESTIONS

1. Why is storytelling important to startups?

2. How do startups get going with storytelling?

3. What are the most important considerations?

4. Why is being customer-centric so important?

5. What is the value of corporate lore?

EXERCISE:

Create a list of stories that your startup could pitch to reporters and bloggers. To make things more interesting (and entertaining!), have people play the roles of a startup entrepreneur pitching a story and a reporter/blogger getting pitched. It is an effective way to quickly see what works and what bombs.

CHAPTER FOUR

What's Your Story, Morning Glory?

"What's your story morning glory?"
- Ella Fitzgerald

When building a house, one of the key elements is a strong foundation. Ideally, the foundation is high quality, flexible and durable in order to support the structure being built on top of it. When it comes to storytelling, the "foundation" is clear messaging that resonates with target audiences about who you are, and, as important, who you are not. Without being too dramatic, messaging sets the stage for everything a startup does - marketing, social media, sales, hiring, and attracting capital. It establishes the "core story" of what a company does, the value its products deliver to users, how it is unique, and why it is better than the competition. Messaging lets a startup identify the best opportunities by focusing on what is important.

Stuart MacDonald, a business advisor, says messaging must be created in the early stages. "Messaging makes things easier by letting you build something that is tailor made, and that feels just right for the targeted audiences or prospective customers you want to service." Without strong messaging, a startup will struggle to gain any kind of traction, even if it has a good product. In competitive and fast-moving markets, messaging is a huge differentiator because it lets a startup rise above the crowd.

But here's the thing: messaging is not easy to create. It can be a challenging and time-consuming process because it forces a startup to boil down its raison d'etre, and how it meets the needs of customers. Creating messaging can also test the key assumptions that a startup has about its product and the opportunity being tackled. In some cases, a startup may have to reload on its vision when messaging challenges a well-entrenched vision. At the end of the messaging process, you are looking to nail the three C's: clarity, coherency and consistency. Strong messaging delivers an easy to understand package of what you do and what is in it for the customer. At the same time, it lets a startup make sure everything it does – marketing, sales, customer service, etc. - is consistent, and every employee is speaking from the same page.

The Messaging Deliverables

A messaging exercise delivers a healthy return on investment because the deliverables can be used to drive marketing and sales activity in a variety of ways. This list includes:

- Unique value propositions that clearly and quickly tell the world what you do, the benefits and the target audiences.
- Brand positioning statement: a short statement on what your product does for customers.
- Key benefits that articulate how customers get value from your products.
- Elevator pitch: A few paragraphs that talk about what your company does, its products and the value being delivered.
- Boilerplate: A 100 to 150 word statement that encapsulates what a company does, the opportunity or problem being addressed, its history and vision, and target audiences.

The 10 commandments of messaging:

1. Embrace outside ideas: It is important to embrace third-party perspective and feedback. This opens the door to ideas and approaches that would otherwise not emerge.
2. Prepare for change: Accepting the status quo makes you vulnerable to new needs and rivals. Messaging is a fluid process that involves continual adjustments.

3. Get uncomfortable: Think out of the box, and resist the urge to rest on your laurels with what you know or what may be currently working.
4. Experiment: Don't be afraid to head off in different directions, even if they end up in dead ends. As Ralph Waldo Emerson said, "All life is an experiment. The more experiments you make the better."
5. Draw a line in the sand. Accept not being perfect. Messaging is an ongoing process that involves big and small iterations. It will never be perfect but that's okay.
6. Test, reload, and test some more: Nothing is created in a silo. Test what you have, make any changes, and keep moving forward.
7. Focus on customers, not product: Always be customer-centric. Put yourselves in your customers' shoes to talk to them rather than at them.
8. Be different and/or unique: Don't be afraid to stand out from the crowd. Study the competition to identify how you can be different.
9. Get key stakeholders involved - employees, customers, investors and partners. Ideas come from everyone so all stakeholders should have a seat at the table.
10. Embrace Kaizen, a Japanese approach to continuous improvement. Always remember messaging can be improved, tweaked or overhauled.

What are the biggest messaging mistakes made by startups?

Messaging is a challenge because it means having a customer-centric view of the world. Messaging involves talking to your customers about their needs and goals, rather than telling customers what your product does. Many startups think that talking about their products and communicating with customers are one and the same, but there are big differences. When a company takes a customer-centric approach, it knows its customers inside and out. It has knowledge about a customer's pains, motivations and needs (which can be great material for stories). Here is something important to remember about customers: in some ways, they do not care about what your product does. All they care about is how your product makes their lives easier, better, more profitable, etc. It is about them, not you.

The biggest thing many startups do not possess when it comes to messaging and storytelling is perspective. They are so focused on the task at hand - building and selling products - it is easy to forget about the outside world. You would think not being cognizant of the world around you is difficult but startups can be self-absorbed environments where developing and selling a product is the biggest priority – in some cases, the only priority. Even when a startup's sales are going well, it often lacks good insight about who is buying its products. Not knowing your audience and their interests makes it difficult, if not impossible, to create stories that resonate. The importance of perspective should not be under-estimated. Too many startups operate in silos or vacuums. Developing their ideas and products is such an inward-looking activity that it is difficult to see the big picture, the needs and interests of customers, and what competitors are doing. Perspective emerges when a startup reaches out to external parties: customers, advisors, investors and the people willing to provide feedback. Do not be alarmed if getting perspective leads to big and small changes in strategic and tactical direction.

KEY TAKEAWAY:

Strong messaging is about providing customers with information about your product and how it meets their needs. It is not about your product.

"What exactly is the key message? It's the one thing you want to tell people about your startup. Think of it as a big, bold, benefits-driven statement that grabs peoples' attention and explains why they should care" - Cezary Pietrzak, marketing and mobile consultant

KEY QUESTIONS:

1. What does your company do?

2. What the biggest benefits from using your products?

3. What's in it for me (the customer)? What value is delivered?

4. Who are the target audiences?

5. What are the key messaging deliverables?

EXERCISE:

See how easily or quickly you can develop messaging. As a group, write down what your startup does, the biggest benefits your products deliver to users, and who is being targeted. Set a time limit of five minutes. Have everyone read their messaging to see the different approaches taken and the common themes. You may be surprised by the diversity.

CHAPTER FIVE

Diving into the Messaging Process

"If you can't explain it simply, you don't understand it well enough"
- **Albert Einstein**

So, how does messaging happen?

One of the realities of running a startup is that you are dealing with a lot of information. This information needs to be unlocked, unleashed and explored to identify the most compelling ideas, topics and themes. It can take many conversations to make this happen; some during formal sessions, and some ad hoc. At times, this may seem like a slow process but messaging gradually unfolds as ideas are pushed into the spotlight and examined. In an ideal world, messaging would happen in a flash but the real world process is more measured and methodical. Cezary Pietrzak, a marketing and mobile consultant, says messaging takes time because it involves defining the brand, and understanding your audience and marketing niche. "You need to generate ideas and themes that deliver insights for what messaging could be."

So how do you start to develop messaging? It is a multi-step process that works like a funnel. It starts with gathering information about your company, product, market and competitors. Then, this information is boiled down into content that succinctly communicates to your customers why your product is the best option for them. "Messaging is hard," Pietrzak says. "You can't do it well if you don't understand the brand, audience and the marketplace. How many startups have defined their audience, defined their brand and figured out how people perceive them and the category? I would suggest very few."

One of the most important components of messaging is having well-defined processes. It does not mean the process has to be rigid and lack flexibility, but it provides the structure to take the right steps along the way. An instructive way to facilitate the messaging process is Pietrzak's Marketing Fundamentals Canvas to develop a company's mission and vision statement, brand, target audiences, market niche and core messaging. It is a user-friendly tool that maps out the key elements.

MISSION		VISION	
The company's purpose + reason for being		The company's long-term business goals	
BRAND	**TARGET AUDIENCE**	**MARKET NICHE**	
A promise the company makes to its customers	The customers that the company serves	The company's position in the market relative to competition	
KEY MESSAGE			*Marketing Fundamentals Canvas*
The one idea the company conveys to its audience			cezary.co

Source: http://www.cezary.co/

Let's go through the different steps of the messaging process:

1. Discovery

Messaging begins with an in-depth exploration of a startup's history, vision, products, customers and competitors. It involves gathering as much information as possible. In other words, it is a brain dump. You want ideas - good, bad or indifferent - to rumble onto the table in all their glory. This is not the time to be timid, intimated or cautious. If messaging is going to be effectively developed, the discovery process needs openness and transparency. It can be an eye-opening exercise because startups have to answer questions that may not have previously been explored or regarded as important.

At this point in the messaging process, it can be valuable to have multiple stakeholders at the table: founders, executives, employees, investors and advisors. It is an opportunity to get a variety of perspectives and ideas that set the stage for the best messaging to materialize. It is better to have too many cooks in the kitchen because you never know who will offer fresh or different thinking. One of the best ways to approach "Discovery" is creating a list of questions that provide structure for in-depth discussions, although you do want the flexibility to explore interesting or thought provoking directions.

What are the key questions?
1. What does our product do?
2. What are the leading benefits?
3. What are the key features?
4. Who are our customers and target audiences (e.g. partners, investors)?
5. What are the characteristics of our ideal customer(s)?
6. What are our customers' biggest points of pain?
7. How do we resolve these pains?
8. How is our product different or unique?
9. Who's the competition – direct and indirect rivals (think QuickBooks versus Excel)?
10. Why would a customer select a competitor's product?
11. Where do we see the company in three to five years?
12. What are our goals for revenue and employees?

By the end of a discovery process, there should be pages and pages of notes. Within this information are nuggets of messaging gold - inspiring ideas, interesting keywords, competitive insight and, hopefully, a complete understanding of a startup's product (e.g. strengths, weaknesses, etc.) and customers.

What is done with all this information?

Aside from having a better sense about a startup, the next step is identifying words, phrases and ideas that get people excited, enthusiastic or intrigued. It could be a single word that triggers a wave of messaging creativity. This step requires patience and a willingness to sift through the proverbial haystack to discover a needle. To help this process move forward, it may be helpful to print your notes to make it easier to find key words, phrases and themes.

2. Discovery

After gathering information from a startup's key stakeholders, the next step is getting information from external stakeholders (aka customers). As we talk about throughout the book, it is important to have a customer-centric approach to create engaging stories. This involves talking to:

- Existing customers: people who have been with your startup for different periods of time. Long-time customers will have distinct perspectives and needs than customers who just joined the fold.
- Potential customers: people currently using a competitive product but looking to upgrade from an old product to a new one (e.g. software vs. online services), or exploring new ways to do business.
- Former customers: people who decided, for whatever reason, your product no longer fit the bill.
- Non-customers who considered a purchase but did not proceed. Getting insight into why they picked another option is invaluable.

You are looking for insight into a customer's needs, points of pain, interests, buying process, and why they selected your product rather than a competitor's. What is it about your company and product they like or want improved? How would they describe your company or product? Would they recommend your product to friends and colleagues? Do not be surprised if customers provide insight that sparks questions or causes you to reconsider key assumptions. It is important to identify the key themes about your product and the competitive landscape so they can be incorporated into the messaging process.

3. Research

As much as the discovery process unearths interesting and thought-provoking themes and ideas, a startup also needs to look at the marketplace and the competitive landscape. This can involve industry research (buyers, sellers, key trends), a SWOT analysis and a competitive audit focused on messaging and how rivals talk about their products and themselves. Some of the ways to do research include:

- An in-depth exploration of a startup's marketplace from a high-level perspective. Why is the market growing? What are the needs and interests of consumers? Who are the market leaders? What companies are falling by the wayside? To do proper research, you need to monitor news coverage, read analyst reports and get a feel for the industry's history.
- A comprehensive review of a startup's marketing and sales collateral. You want to get a better handle about a startup's product, market and its existing story. Some of the collateral may be incoherent or lack focus, but there may be things that resonate or stand out as effective, interesting or compelling. Even if there are only a few interesting items, they can become valuable building blocks.

4. Competitive Analysis

In this step, the focus turns to a startup's leading rivals. These can be direct (Google vs. Bing) or indirect (QuickBooks vs. Excel). From a storytelling perspective, you want to get a feel for how rivals communicate and talk about themselves, the language and keywords used, and the different channels to do marketing and storytelling. This research delivers valuable context and information about the competitive landscape, and how a startup can position itself in a unique or different way.

To get a feel for the competition, here is a list of what to review:

- Websites: Explore and record the language and words used on competitors' Websites to understand the things seen as important or emphasized. Get a feel for the overall tone. Is it confident, bold or friendly? Identify things that stand out or come across as interesting or unique. Take a look at blog posts to see their focus, the topics being discussed and the tone. Want more competitive insight? Sign up for a rival's newsletters, listen to their Webinars, read their case studies, and watch their videos.
- Media and blog coverage: Look at the coverage that competitors have attracted, the most common storylines (e.g. financing, new features, customer milestones, partnerships), and the media organizations and blogs providing coverage. Write down the most common themes and ideas.
- Industry reports. Getting access to industry research can generate a treasure trove of information, context and competitive analysis. The research may not mention your startup, but it will provide guidance interesting trends or popular industry words and terms. Some reports will have a competitive analysis, including a segmentation based on different parameters such as pricing, market

focus and features.
- Social media: You can get a good handle on a startup's brand personality from social media activity on platforms such as Twitter, Facebook, YouTube, LinkedIn and Pinterest. By looking at tweets, updates, etc., it is easier to see how a startup and its rivals communicate, the type of things discussed, and the language used. Tools such as TweetDeck, Hootsuite and Topsy can quickly surface lots of valuable insight.

To provide context, create a mind map (digital or paper-based) that includes your company and the competition. Then, write down the key words, phrases and ideas for each rival. This could include looking at their value propositions, key benefits and "About" pages. With all the key rivals in place, it should provide a good sense of how everyone is positioned.

Here is a mind map that I developed for a client, OnCall, which was looking to position its mobile ask-an-expert service against rivals. The mind map included direct and indirect rivals, and then placed them in different quadrants based four parameters. The exercise made it easier for OnCall to not only create unique messaging but also determine its biggest rivals.

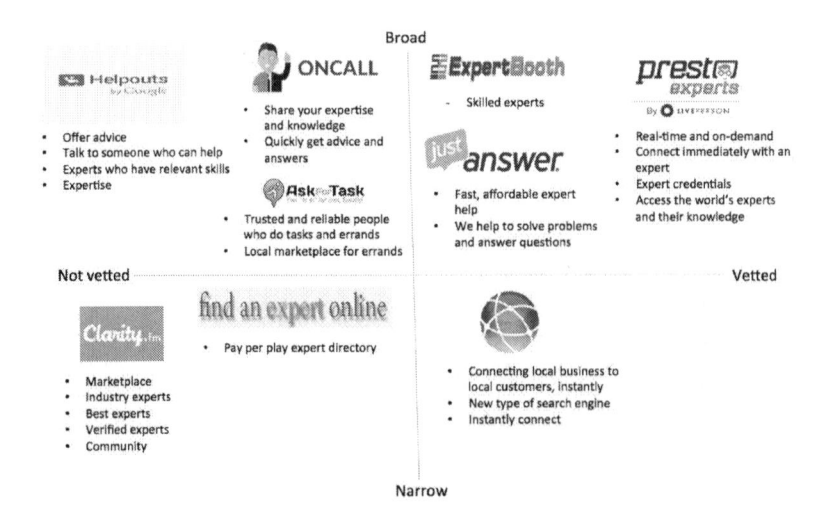

Broad

Helpouts by Google
- Offer advice
- Talk to someone who can help
- Experts who have relevant skills
- Expertise

ONCALL
- Share your expertise and knowledge
- Quickly get advice and answers

AskTask
- Trusted and reliable people who do tasks and errands
- Local marketplace for errands

ExpertBooth
- Skilled experts

justanswer
- Fast, affordable expert help
- We help to solve problems and answer questions

presto experts By LivePerson
- Real-time and on-demand
- Connect immediately with an expert
- Expert credentials
- Access the world's experts and their knowledge

Not vetted ── Vetted

Clarity.fm
- Marketplace
- Industry experts
- Best experts
- Verified experts
- Community

find an expert online
- Pay per play expert directory

- Connecting local business to local customers, instantly
- New type of search engine
- Instantly connect

Narrow

Standing out from the crowd

In a competitive landscape, one of the most important considerations is standing out from the crowd. For startups, this is crucial because the barriers to entry are relatively low, and rivals can quickly replicate new or innovative ideas. It means startups must identify how they are unique and different to position their brand and carve out a competitive edge, even if that edge is minor. If this can't be achieved, a startup risks coming across as just another me-too product.

How do startups discover what makes them different or unique?

It begins with diving into the competitive landscape to look at how rivals position themselves. Who rises above the crowd, and how do they do it? What are the things every competitor claims – e.g. our products are user-friendly, intuitive, efficient, etc.? To get a better grasp of where everyone sits, it helps to create a graph that places companies in different buckets (e.g. free, freemium, premium, SMB, etc.) When exploring ways to be different, accepting risk is part of the process. Playing it safe with your brand/product and how it is positioned is often the path of least resistance. If you want customers to only say good things, you are not going to take any chances or risk going against the grain. But if you want to generate a strong reaction - good or bad - it means stepping out of your comfort zone. Embracing risk means taking storytelling to the next level creatively. Sometimes, these stories are mega-successes; sometimes, they are failures. But this approach offers huge potential to outflank competitors that play it safe.

In his book *"Zag"*, Marty Neumeier talks about the need to

be "really different" to create a product that will enjoy a large brand presence and major profits. To help companies get a sense of how to be different, Neumeier uses an axis with "good" and "different" as the two characteristics. The ideal place to be, he says, is "good and different". He cites examples such as Toyota Prius, Cirque du Soleil and the Aeron chair as examples. Neumeier says what is interesting about the "good and different" quadrant is sometimes these products do not fare well in tests and have difficulty when they hit the market. It could be that consumers believe they are happy with the status quo, or perhaps they are not, in fact, ready for something new and different. In time, Neumeier, says these products thrive because consumers start to equate "different" with "good", which earns them large market share and strong brand potential.

Still, Neumeier says good and different can be a challenging proposition given potential winners can often look like dogs because success hinges on consumers being able to accept, rather than reject, different. He uses the Mini Cooper as an example. Even though research showed U.S. consumers were more interested in SUVs than small cars, BMW launched the Mini Cooper. Neumeier says BMW's decision was counter-intuitive, but this approach allowed it to successfully find "open market space".

STORYTELLING FOR STARTUPS 51

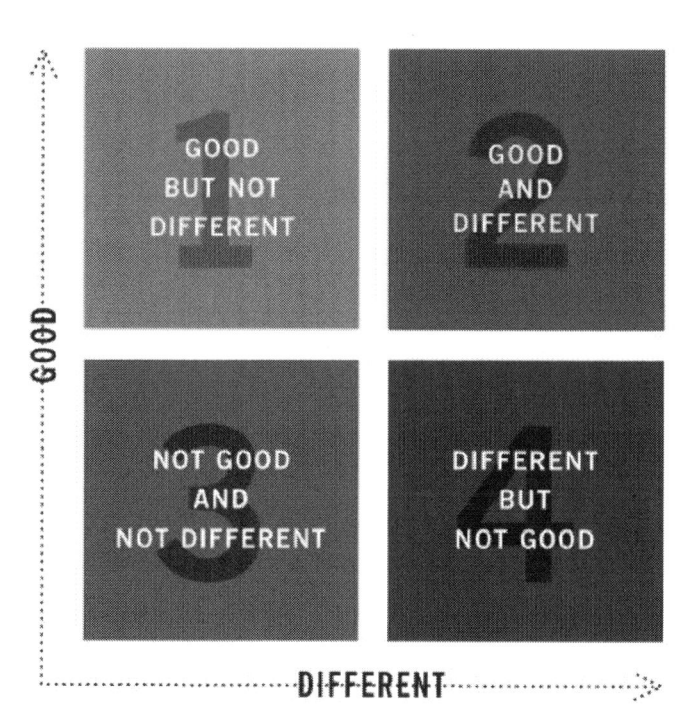

GOOD BUT NOT DIFFERENT	GOOD AND DIFFERENT
NOT GOOD AND NOT DIFFERENT	DIFFERENT BUT NOT GOOD

GOOD (vertical axis) / **DIFFERENT** (horizontal axis)

1 GOOD BUT NOT DIFFERENT
- Does very well in tests
- Goes to market easily
- Generates incremental profits until challenged by competitors
- Earns no market share
- Some brand potential

2 GOOD AND DIFFERENT
- Does poorly in tests
- Goes to market w/ difficulty
- Customers soon equate "different" with "good"
- Generates lasting profits
- Earns large market share
- Strong brand potential

3 NOT GOOD AND NOT DIFFERENT
- Does well in tests
- Goes to market easily
- Generates incremental profits but eventually fails in marketplace
- Earns small market share
- Little brand potential

4 DIFFERENT BUT NOT GOOD
- Does poorly in tests
- Goes to market w/ difficulty
- Eventually fails in marketplace as customers equate "different" with "bad"
- Earns no market share
- No brand potential

Source: http://www.liquidagency.com/zagbook/

CASE STUDY: ESTABLISHING UNIQUE POSITIONING

A good example of a startup that successfully established unique positioning is 500px.com, which plays in the ultra-competitive photo-sharing market. So how does a startup find a place where it can be seen as different? For 500px, the magic happened when it decided to position itself as *the* place for photographers to display their most beautiful photographs. By positioning the brand in this way, 500px created a unique place for itself. In the process, it attracted well-known and high-quality photographers who liked the idea of having a place for their best shots. This, in turn, generated significant buzz, which enticed more photographers who wanted to be part of the 500px community.

Evgeny Tchebotarev, 500px's co-founder, said being different was something that came easily when the company launched in 2004 as a blog. At the time, there was no Flickr, Facebook or Instagram so simply being a photo-sharing site was different. As more competitors emerged, he says 500px's decision to become the place to share beautiful photographs was a natural transition. "Being different helped a lot, especially when Facebook and Flickr were focused on sheer numbers," Tchebotarev says. "There were only so many things we could compete on, so we competed on quality. It gave us an advantage because we were able to say, 'upload your party photos to Facebook, your professional photos to Flickr, and your best photos to 500px'."

A key takeaway from 500px is that a startup does not have to be significantly different or unique; it just needs to have a slant, angle or approach that is not like everyone else. In many ways, 500px has the same features as other photo-sharing services, but its ability to stand out from the crowd created the impression it is truly unique.

Bottom line: It is not easy to be unique or different but it is a competitive necessity if a startup wants to avoid strategies such as relying on low prices or spending a lot of money on advertising. It means spending the time and energy to focus on how you are unique and different. Do your homework, do lots of research, talk to potential and existing customers, bounce ideas off people who do not have a vested interest in your startup, brainstorm and experiment. At some point, you may hit the jackpot when the things that make you unique bubble to the surface.

5. Brainstorming

After the discovery, research and competitive analysis processes are completed, several themes or ideas should emerge as the most interesting or having the biggest potential. These are important building blocks upon which messaging can be developed. At this point, you are looking to embrace a focused approach that will move ideas forward. The best way to approach brainstorming is having in-depth discussions about specific words, phrases, topics and ideas. This is a litmus test for the time and work that has already gone into the messaging process. In an ideal world, everything identified as having potential is embraced and developed. But the reality is often different. While some ideas generate excitement, other ideas solicit, at best, a "meh" (aka not encouraging or inspiring).

What are the keys to effective brainstorming?

1. Be clear about the problem being tackled. Ralph Keeney, a professor at Duke University's Fuqua School Business, who specializes in brainstorming, says this provides

much-needed focus and a path to better solutions and answers.
2. People need to be fired up and engaged. Their willingness to bring energy to the table is a huge ingredient for success.
3. Invite people who really want to be there and, as important, who are not afraid to express their opinions. In other words, no wallflowers.
4. Be open to all kinds of ideas: good, indifferent and bad. Having different angles and approaches makes for dynamic brainstorming.
5. There can be no distractions – no smartphones, computers, food or interruptions. Ask everyone to be focused for a set amount of time (e.g. an hour) so you can get their best efforts.
6. Be clear about what the brainstorming session will deliver. This gives people a better sense of what needs to be achieved.
7. Have someone facilitate the session to provide structure, maintain a good flow, get everyone involved, and ensure interesting ideas are properly explored.

How can you tell if a brainstorming session is working?

During good brainstorming sessions, lots of ideas, opinions and questions are discussed. Using a whiteboard or easels with paper is a good way to track the discussion and help people visualize concepts and ideas. You want people engaged so they offer their thoughts, criticisms and guidance, as well as having ideas scrutinized, tested and strengthened. Be prepared for people to disagree, propose strange or different concepts, or not be as engaged as they should. This is part of the process. At some point during a brainstorming session, specific ideas, phrases or concepts will start to emerge – something a facilitator can galvanize. Then, the brainstorming becomes more focused so the most promising ideas can be embraced and supported.

From the discovery, market research and brainstorming stages, you are looking for key themes and topics upon which to build messaging. In many cases, phrases and words emerge that capture the essence of your startup's product, customers and mission. I have worked with clients where entire concepts have rumbled into the spotlight, as well as clients where only one keyword pops up.

MESSAGING CASE STUDY

A good example of how brainstorming happens in strange ways is work I did with Vigorate, a Toronto-based digital marketing agency. After wading through a lot of information and exploring the competitive landscape, all my brainstorming ideas were summarily rejected..... except for one word: "performance".

For whatever reason, the people around the table liked "performance" because it underscored the different kinds of work the agency did for clients. It was a word they could rally around because it captured how they operated. By focusing on a single word, they were to able drive forward messaging with an idea that quickly and enthusiastically had everyone on the same page. It involved taking one step backward and then two steps forward because it was a new concept to embrace, but "performance" ended up being the critical element for a successful messaging exercise. "Because we could see the change in the market, we knew we had to adapt in some way," explained Michael Grieve,

Vigorate's CEO. "Everyone was quite open to trying to define it, and I think we were able to identify something that had commonality with everyone."

Vigorate's path to messaging illustrates how messaging can be a strange journey that zigzags and rambles off into different directions as opposed to being a linear process. At some point, the finish line appears, although perhaps not in the fashion originally expected.

6. Draft Messaging

The next step is creating a draft version of "the story". In working with startups, I like to establish the foundation for messaging with a 75 to 125-word statement that describes what a startup does, the target audiences being served and the value its products deliver to customers. This approach provides a startup with something tangible to review and discuss. It is important to appreciate that it is not a negative if the draft messaging does not strike a perfect chord with everyone. In an ideal world, it is would be great if everyone loved the draft messaging but it usually does not happen. At this point, people still have preconceived notions or biases about a startup's focus, products and markets, so expect pushback. It is important to take the time to digest the draft messaging, rather than reacting immediately. Once people have had time to think about it, they can come back to the table to go through the positives and negatives.

With a draft of "the story" created, you can start shaping it into different messaging vehicles: value propositions, positioning statements, elevator pitches and boilerplates. (Note: We will explore these vehicles in the next chapter.)

7. Testing

The testing of messaging is a crucial part of the process. A startup is looking for feedback about the clarity, tone and personality of the key words and messaging. Startups need to be careful about not having a misalignment between their messaging and the markets in which they operate. When I worked with one startup, they wanted their messaging to be fun, cheeky and somewhat irreverent to differentiate themselves from their Big Data competitors. But when they showed the messaging to an advisor, they were told the language completely missed the mark because their potential customers were large enterprises that wanted to deal with companies that were solid, not fun.

Some of the ways to test messaging include:
- Focus groups that involve different kinds of people – potential customers, existing customers, people with little knowledge about your company or industry, etc.
- Online services such as Feedback Army (feedback-army.com), UserTesting (usertesting.com) or Applause (applause.com), which offer an easy way to get feedback from a global audience.
- Facebook advertising: Create ads with different versions of your messaging to see which ones attract the most clicks. This approach is particularly valuable for early-stage startups looking for messaging and product

validation. This is a relatively inexpensive exercise because you pay only when someone clicks on an ad. If no one clicks on an ad, you probably have a messaging problem.

8. Iterations

From feedback and testing, a startup will come to a point where messaging works for everyone. It may not be perfect but it passes the sniff test from everyone involved. This is a positive but it is also a starting point, rather than the finish line. As a startup grows, customer needs evolve and new competitors emerge, the messaging needs to continually be tweaked to stay current, effective and vibrant. It means having processes to review messaging on a regular basis. One of the ways to drive iterations is having monthly update sessions to discuss new developments (new features, questions raised by customers, etc.) and the competitive landscape (what is being done by rivals, new players, etc.)

KEY TAKEAWAY:

One of the important things to remember with messaging is it is not always a smooth-running process given stakeholders have different ideas and expectations.

"Everyone's desire to be right is always going to be in conflict with where you want to go. The key is looking at where you're stuck, and being able to talk about it. The second you can talk about it, there is so much power once the group starts working well together, it will give birth to whatever it is you are trying to achieve. It is not a mathematical exercise or a factual exercise, but a purely emotional exercise." - Michael Grieve, CEO and senior partner, Vigorate Digital

KEY QUESTIONS:

1. How does the messaging process start?

2. What are the key steps along the way?

3. Who should be involved in the messaging process?

4. How is the effectiveness of your messaging tested?

5. What are the key messaging deliverables?

EXERCISE

Create a mind map that includes your leading rivals – direct and indirect. For each company, write down the words and phrases used on their Websites, particularly the home and About pages. Do the same for your company. This will provide interesting context into how each company communicates and whether your company's language is similar or different.

To guide you through the messaging process, the workbook on the next page puts the spotlight on some of the key areas for discovery and discussion.

Mission Statement
Why does our organization exist?
• What is your vision?
• What problem is being tackled?

Vision Statement
• What do you hope that you, and your stakeholders/target customers will accomplish in the future?

Corporate Goals
• Where do you see the company in three to five years?
• How many employees?
• How much revenue?

Product
• What products does your company offer?
• How is your product unique, better or different?
• What are the leading benefits?
• What are the key features?

Target Audiences
• Who are your customers and other target audiences (e.g. partners, investors)?
• What are the leading characteristics of your core customer(s)?
• What are their biggest points of pain?
• How does your startup resolve these pains?
• How do customers research product options?
• What are the biggest purchase factors?

Competitive Positioning
• Who is the competition? This includes direct rivals (e.g. Google Docs vs. Dropbox) or indirect rivals (e.g. QuickBooks vs. Excel)
• Who are the top-three direct competitors?
• What are their services and attributes?
• Why would customers pick them over your products?

Reputation Assessment
• What adjectives describe your business?
• How would customers describe your business?
• What keywords and phrases resonate with each of your audiences?
• How would they describe your competitors?

CHAPTER SIX

Messaging Deliverables

"Ideas are easy. Implementation is hard."

- **Guy Kawasaki**, entrepreneur

Okay, you have survived the messaging process. Congratulations! Give yourself a big pat on the back because, for the most part, the hard work is done. The messaging process is grunt work, but it is a matter of short-term pain, long-term gain. Messaging is a necessary evil because it forces a startup to examine and scrutinize its products, marketplace and competitors. It puts the spotlight on questions, challenges, opportunities and concerns, and identifies strengths and weaknesses. At this point, you are probably saying: "Yeah, this is all good but what does messaging deliver to drive my startup forward?" Here is a list of the things that come out of messaging:

- Value propositions
- Positioning statement
- Boilerplate
- Elevator pitch

The messaging "dividends" are invaluable because they are the key building blocks to drive a startup's marketing and sales activities. They provide startups with a super-clear idea about how they meet the needs of customers. As important, good messaging and content sets the stage for a startup's marketing and sales efforts to be planned and developed in a coherent and consistent way.

So, let's get into each part on the list to provide insight into what they are, how to create them, and their value.

VALUE PROPOSITIONS

Value propositions are one of the most valuable parts of a messaging exercise. Value propositions are short but powerful statements that communicate the value/benefits of your product and how it solves a customer's problem or points of pain.

Another definition comes from marketing consultant Neil Patel, who defines a value proposition as a "sentence that tells your visitors why they should buy from you and not your competitors." Value propositions answer a key question: "What's it in for me?" that customers want answered by your marketing and sales collateral. If you are not taking a customer-centric approach, it is difficult to answer the question.

Effective value propositions move customers into the sales funnel because they offer reasons to buy your products. You may be thinking that value propositions should be easy to create because they are short and sweet. But this is often not the case. For one, value propositions need to encapsulate a lot of information. They need to tell people what you do and articulate how you are different or unique. In a fast-moving world, value propositions capture someone's attention - no mean feat - so you can offer them more information. Value propositions make you focus on your best benefits and features. These make potential customers say, "This product looks interesting, I want to learn more about it". Ideally, value propositions give your company and products an unfair advantage.

A key part of value propositions is uniqueness. What is it about your products that stand out from the crowd? It could be lower prices, ease of use, excellent customer service, faster shipping, availability (e.g. beta or exclusive offers), the ability to customize it, or how it is a better solution than everything else on the market.

How are value propositions created?

It is not a complicated process, but it takes time to do right. It starts with getting a strong handle on your customers. What are their key characteristics, buying habits, needs, pains, interests and motivations? What products are they currently using, and what are their shortcomings? If they switched to a new product, what are the risks and hurdles that would encumber them? Why would they want your product? In other words, it is an in-depth exercise that delivers a lot of insight into what resonates with customers.

An efficient way to create valuable propositions is splitting the exercise into two parts: the product and the customer. The graphic below created by Peter J. Thomson, a digital brand strategist, does an excellent job of highlighting both sides of the equation. It makes it easy to answer important questions around what your product does, what it feels like to use your product, and how your product works. In looking at customers, the graphic makes you focus on a buyer's needs, emotional and rational drivers, and the products currently being used.

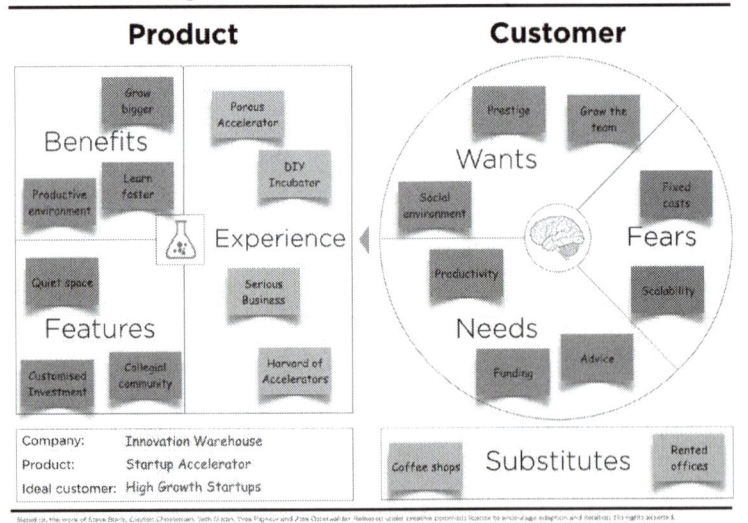

Source: http://www.peterjthomson.com/2013/11/value-proposition-canvas/value-proposition-canvas-example-iw

Another critical element is looking at your product.

- What are the strengths?
- What are the weaknesses?
- How is it unique or different?
- What are the most attractive features?
- Is it user-friendly or difficult to embrace?
- How much training does it take to be successful?
- How it is better or worse than the competition?

Asking these questions will let the most interesting, relevant and compelling ideas rise to the surface. It puts the spotlight on your product's advantages, differences and how it connects with consumers looking to make their lives easier, more productive, more profitable, fun, etc.

Let's take a look at some good value propositions:

shopify	*Shopify is everything you need to sell everywhere.* Why it works: Abundantly clear what Shopify does and offers
optimizely	*A/B testing you'll actually use* *One optimization platform for Websites and mobile apps.* Why it works: Short and sweet but clear about what Optimizely does and, as important, an emphasis on how it is unique.

unbounce	*Build, publish & A/B testing landing pages with I.T. The mobile responsive landing page builder for marketers.* Why it works: There is no confusion what Unbounce delivers, and why it is easy for customers to embrace.
Yanado	*Task management inside Gmail. Manage your work without leaving your Gmail.* Why it works: A concise way to tell people what Yanado does and how it is used.
mint.com	*Be good with your money. See your bills and finances in one place, and do more with your money every day.* Why it works: It leaves no doubt about Mint's value and why someone would use it.

How to tell if your value propositions are effective?

The best way to discover whether your value propositions work is simple: do lots of testing. It can involve A/B testing by using different value propositions to see which one generates the best response. You want people to spend as little time as possible thinking about what your startup does and why it is interesting. There should be no confusion or guesswork. You know a value proposition works when someone quickly nods their head (aka they get what you do), and then wants to learn more.

BRANDING POSITIONING STATEMENT

What does your startup do for the customer? If you can answer that question using a handful of words, the chances of convincing a customer to consider your product are tremendously enhanced.

Positioning statements are short, snappy and clear statements about what a startup does. They are customer-centric, talking about the benefits that a customer receives from your product. A strong positioning statement sparks curiosity and interest. It sets the stage for someone to learn more about your startup. Here is an example: "Netflix is the best service to watch videos because it delivers a huge selection of on-demand content that meet the needs of different consumers".

That is a lot of pressure for a small number of words that take seconds to read, but it illustrates the importance of a positioning statement in a world that sees multi-tasking and time-strapped customers make snap decisions. If a positioning statement fails to rock the house, it does not matter if your startup's product has great benefits and plenty of features. In the scheme of things, the positioning statement is one of the most challenging things for a startup to develop because so much information needs to be squeezed into so little space.

Here are two approaches to create position statements. The common elements are a focus on the target audience, the value delivered and how it is different or unique:

In "Crossing the Chasm", Geoffrey Moore created this template for value positioning.

For _____(target customer)_____

Who _____(statement of need or opportunity)_____,

___(Product name)_____ **is a** _____(product category)_____

That _____(statement of key benefit)_____.

Unlike _____(competing alternative)_____

_____(Product name)(statement of differentiation)_____.

A similar approach is Adeo Ressi's "Madlibs" technique:

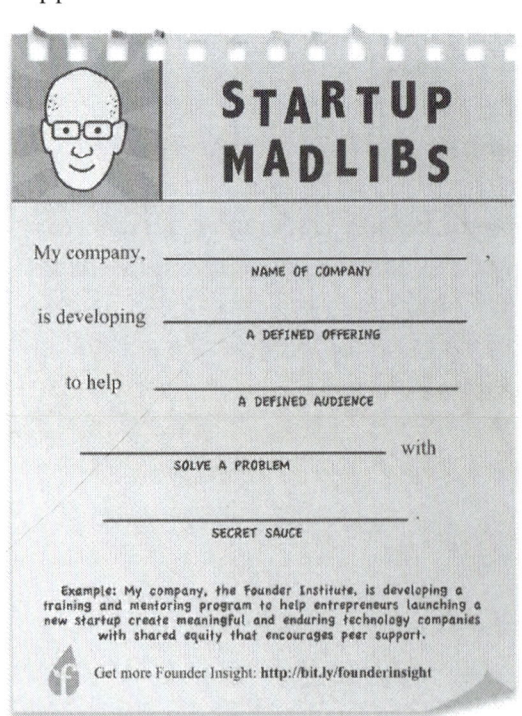

STARTUP MADLIBS

My company, _____,
                 NAME OF COMPANY

is developing _____
                A DEFINED OFFERING

to help _____
           A DEFINED AUDIENCE

_____ with
    SOLVE A PROBLEM

_____.
    SECRET SAUCE

Example: My company, the Founder Institute, is developing a training and mentoring program to help entrepreneurs launching a new startup create meaningful and enduring technology companies with shared equity that encourages peer support.

Get more Founder Insight: http://bit.ly/founderinsight

Source: fi.co/madlibs

Here is an example of how a brand positioning statement could be constructed using Startup Madlibs:

Amazon is a retail bookseller
That provides instant access to over 1.1 million books.
Unlike traditional book retailers,
Amazon provides a combination of extraordinary convenience, low prices and comprehensive selection.

ELEVATOR PITCH

What do you do?

It is a simple but loaded question that every entrepreneur has to nail. The answer needs to be concise, convincing and intriguing, and the audience has to easily grasp it. In other words, it is not an easy task.

An elevator pitch is one or two sentences that make it easy for people to get what you do. You are packing a lot of information into a 30-second statement so elevator pitches are challenging to create. But having a powerful elevator pitch sparks conversations and questions, and gets your foot in the door. Being clear about what your products do and the benefits delivered can be the difference between leads/sales or an empty pipeline, and attracting investors or going home empty.

What are the keys to an effective elevator pitch?

It starts by being as simple and to-the-point as possible. We do/make "X" that helps customers do "Y". It is a sentence anyone can immediately understand. There are no industry acronyms or lingo. Again, think simple because we live in a fast-moving world in which people do not want to work to understand what your company does. Make it a snap to grasp, so stay away from buzzwords and industry vernacular. To help with the creation of elevator pitches, a useful tool is PitchGrub (pitchgrub.com).

Second, make it clear how your product serves target audiences. What problems does it solve? Who should use it? How does it make their lives easier, better or more profitable? How would it make them look like a star to friends, colleagues or their boss? A good exercise is flipping the lens to answer the question "What's in it for me?" that potential customers will ask. What do they get from using your product, as opposed to what you want to tell them?

Third, think about adding some sizzle by showing how your product is different from the competition. It does not have to be a multi-pronged, technical kind of thing, but a sentence that says why your product stands out from the crowd. Again, it is not about blowing your horn but making it obvious to users that you are not just selling another widget.

From personal experience, top-notch elevator pitches are deemed successful by the number of head nods, leads and sales generated. By telling your elevator pitch to enough people, you can create a large army of evangelists or marketers who start selling for you. When inbound leads from people you don't know flow into your inbox, it is a sign your "sales team" is doing its job.

Finally, test your elevator pitch. In fact, play with different versions to see what resonates the best. You want to see if different types of people – friends, strangers, customers, employees and investors - understand what you do, the benefits and why someone would care. If you have to explain your elevator pitch because someone does not quickly get it, there is work to do. If, on the other hand, someone gets your elevator pitch, and it sparks questions and requests for more information, you are onto something.

Here is an example of how not to do an elevator pitch:

"Our widget is the market's most user-friendly, and cost-effective. It offers a large number of great features that drive synergies and productivity."

And here is a better way to do it:

"We make widgets that help people save money because they can be easily be installed and maintained."

The differences are subtle, but dramatic. The first pitch has everything to do with the product, while the second is focused on the value for the customer.

BOILERPLATE

It is puzzling to see startups with confusing or bad "About" pages. About pages are the most public opportunity for a startup to provide a clear, interesting and informative picture of what they do, how they are different and their story. Far too often, startups try to be creative when crafting "About" pages, rather than taking a straightforward approach that gives people a quick corporate snapshot. At the heart of a good "About" page is the boilerplate. From a high level, it is a document with six or seven paragraphs, or 150 to 200 words that includes the following elements:

1. What a startup does
2. The benefits it delivers
3. Its strengths and how it is unique - e.g. innovative, award-winning
4. The customers it serves

5. A mini-story of who's behind the startup and how it came to be

A boilerplate is a jargon-free creature that serves as a "workhorse" that makes a startup look credible and the real deal. The boilerplate needs to be accessible because it is read by a variety of people: potential customers, media, analysts, investors, customers, employees and partners.

How do you create a boilerplate?

Think of the boilerplate as an extended story when someone asks what your startup does. It lets you inject personality and an upbeat tone when talking about the product and who should use it, and provide information and context about why your startup was created and who is involved. In a small package, it provides people with a lot of information.

Here is a good example from Copyblogger Media of a boilerplate that tells a great story about its product and history.

We Don't Just Teach Content Marketing ... We Built Our Company With It

> The bible of content marketing ~ VentureBeat

Since January 2006, Copyblogger has been teaching people how to create killer online content. Not bland corporate crap created to fill up a company webpage. *Valuable* information that attracts attention, drives traffic, and builds your business.

These days, that's called content marketing. Copyblogger founder Brian Clark has been building businesses with online content marketing since 1998, before anyone used that term.

Source: www.copyblogger.com/about

KEY TAKEAWAY:

One of the biggest benefits of a messaging exercise is the deliverables, which play a key part in establishing a marketing and sales foundation.

"Messaging is hard. Messaging is being able to develop strong ideas and insights. Messaging is how you express things in the world. Through different channels, you need to nail it." - Cezary Pietrzak

KEY QUESTIONS:

1. What are the different parts of the messaging process?

2. How can messaging be created, tested and iterated?

3. How are value propositions created?

4. What are the questions that need to be asked?

5. Who should be involved in the creation of messaging?

EXERCISE:

Use Adeo Ressi's "Madlibs" technique (fi.co/madlibs) to create a positioning statement, or Pitch-Grub.com to develop an elevator pitch. This is an excellent group exercise to generate different ideas and approaches.

CHAPTER SEVEN
Discovering The Audience For Your Stories

"Companies that do really well tend to have a really deep and, frankly, compassionate or empathetic understanding of their customers. They have clear understanding about who their customers are."

- Stuart MacDonald, business advisor.

Stories work when they are told to the right audiences at the right time. It is a straightforward proposition, right? But defining your audience needs to be more than broad generalizations (e.g. teenagers or married women) or educated guesses….at least it should be if you are serious about delivering stories that resonate and get people to take an action ("story doing") - visit your store, make a purchase, download a white paper, subscribe to a newsletter or call a salesperson.

Discovering, identifying and having a clear understanding of your target audiences has everything do with aligning your product with the people who would be interested in buying or using it. Some of the things you need to know include: What are their problems, challenges and goals? How do they research purchase decisions, and what are the triggers to make a purchase? This involves research and, frankly, grunt work to understand the dynamics and behaviour of customers on your radar. To tell stories successfully, you need an excellent picture of the people who are crucial to the growth of your brand and sales of your products. This process is broken down into two key components: target audiences and buyer personas.

Identifying target audiences

In creating a new product, startups need to focus on fundamentals such as solving a problem or addressing a need in a new or different way. Once a need has been identified, the focus shifts to building the product and making sure it has enough features (aka bells and whistles) to make it interesting to enough consumers.

Surprisingly, a lot of this activity happens with little insight into the people who would purchase the product. Instead, startups embrace the "if you build it, they will come" approach that only works in fictional stories such as *"Field of Dreams"* - the film in which Ray Kinsella (played by Kevin Costner in the Academy Award-nominated movie) builds a baseball diamond in the fields of an Iowa farm. The "if you build it, they will come" approach works in Hollywood but it spells disaster for startups that believe just having an interesting product will get people to beat a path to their door.

Neil Bhapkar, chief marketing officer with FlightNetwork.com, said one of the biggest challenges for startups is over-estimating the size of their audience. As eternal optimists, he says startup entrepreneurs believe their product is so good that everyone should use it. "Instead of understanding it is not for everyone, they try to sell it to everyone. A company with an IT tool will think that every company in the world will use it. The reality is it is a lot trickier than that. By trying to go after the entire market, the story becomes tough during the early stages for a startup."

A better and more pragmatic approach is identifying the customers who could buy or be interested in a startup's product (aka as target audiences). At a high level, target audiences can be defined as "the intended group for which something is performed or marketed; the specific group to which advertising is directed". For example, the target audience for accounting software could be people who want to organize and manage their finances to operate their businesses more efficiently. This is a good starting point to create messaging to drive marketing and sales. In most cases, however, there needs to be a more granular approach to target audiences. Why? Products can appeal to a variety of buyers with a variety of needs and goals. It means a one-size-fits-all marketing and sales approach may not work because it does not reflect that customers come in different shapes and sizes.

To get a strong handle on target audiences, startups need

to identify the different types of buyers from a demographic and psychographic perspective. These buyers can be divided by gender, age, lifestyle, income, interests, values, hobbies, etc. You will discover small but important differences that impact how the product is pitched and sold. By identifying target audiences, it is easier to capture someone's attention because their specific needs and goals are obvious to them.

For any business, including startups, this process takes time, effort and research but it offers invaluable insight into the needs and motivations of customers. For many startups, there can be several target audiences. There are, of course, customers who purchase products. Target audiences can also include potential employees, partners, media/bloggers and investors. Target audiences have different interests and needs, so it is important to recognize the kind of stories that will resonate.

Here is a simple example of how target audiences can be broken down. At a high level, a hotel's target audiences are people looking for a place to stay overnight. But within that target audience, there could be four distinct groups: businesspeople, out-of-town tourists, locals looking for a mini-vacation, and event planners putting together a major conference. Each group is interested in accommodation but they have different needs and interests. A businessperson may want early breakfast service and being close to clients. A tourist is looking for good amenities (gym, pool, shopping) and proximity to leading attractions. A local is looking for a place to relax and dine. And an event planner needs meeting rooms and catering. Identifying target audiences is essential because it identifies the most promising customers. In other words, it is a great way to focus resources and budgets to efficiently drive the business forward.

CASE STUDY: TARGET AUDIENCES

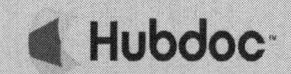

When Jamie Schulman and Jamie McDonald started Hubdoc in 2013, they saw an opportunity to accelerate the adoption of e-bills. With companies spending a lot of money creating and sending paper bills, Schulman and McDonald figured utilities, banks, cable companies and telephone companies would be willing to pay Hubdoc a fee to drive higher e-bill penetration. At least, that was the hypothesis as they worked to attract consumers to use an online service that would aggregate all their bills in one place, while trying to attract companies that would pay Hubdoc for helping to promote e-bills.

Unfortunately, the hypothesis did not work for a simple reason: there were not enough companies willing to pay Hubdoc for getting customers to switch to e-bills from paper. The companies liked the concept and there were many meetings to talk about how it could work, but the deals took a long time to materialize. It was a difficult situation for Schulman and McDonald, who believed they were onto something but could not turn their idea into a vibrant business.

With little sales traction, Hubdoc looked at its "power users", the people who were enthusiastically using the service. They discovered power users were not only using Hubdoc for utilities, telephone, bank and cable bills but also asking if the company could add services such as Google AdWords and GoDaddy. Schulman and McDonald also discovered many of their users were small business owners, consultants and bookkeepers who wanted to use Hubdoc to serve multiple clients. Even better, these were people willing to pay to use Hubdoc.

Schulman said while attracting business owners had always been part of Hubdoc's plan, it was not initially embraced because it did not seem like business owners would pay for the service. Armed

> with new insight about target audiences, Hubdoc now charges customers $20/month for unlimited usage.
> What were the key lessons that Schulman learned along the way? "It is cliché but I believe in customer development. " he says. "Get out as much as you can to talk to people to find out exactly about their pain points. A lot of startups are trying to sell vitamins, rather than painkillers. You can have a slick product that people love and it looks and performs great but do people really need it? Customer development tells you if your customers are in pain or whether they think it's cool but won't pay for it. At the end of the day, you have to get paid and you need revenue that exceeds your costs. The key lesson is get out of the office and talk to people. Pay attention, always have your eyes open, and don't get married to what you think is right."

Buyer Persona Creation

To really know your customers, buyer personas need to be created. While some startups may identify target audiences, they do not drill down into their customers to create detailed buyer personas. Buyer personas are invaluable because they provide granular information about different groups of customers and provide a list of questions that someone might have during the buying process. This information lets a startup create targeted and focused marketing and sales programs. Not to be overly dramatic but buyer personas can be the difference between making a sale and failing to make an impression.

Randy Frisch, chief operating officer with Uberflip, which provides brands with a content marketing platform, says buyer personas address a fundamental need: they make it easier to understand your buyers. It sounds like a straightforward concept but Frisch says many startups overlook buyer personas because they are so product-focused. "In marketing school, you're taught the four P's: price, product, promotion and place. But these have to do with what you're selling, not who you're selling to. Customer personas help you figure out who's on the other side. A customer persona is something that everyone in the company needs to understand so they can rally behind the product."

> **The Four P's of Storytelling**
>
> There are four P's for marketing, but what about storytelling?
> - **People**: Customers are people with needs, problems and goals. They are the people who will hear your stories.
> - **Passion**: While not every product gets consumers excited, people can be passionate when it comes to products that align with their interests.
> - **Purpose**: People buy products for a reason. They want to make their lives more efficient, productive, profitable or easier.
> - **Product**: As much as storytelling drives emotions, it is about selling product. Let's be clear about what needs to happen at the end of the story.

How are buyer personas defined?

According to HubSpot, a popular inbound marketing and sales platform, a buyer persona is a: *"semi-fictional representation of your ideal customer based on market research and real data about your existing customers. When creating your buyer persona(s), consider including customer demographics, behaviour patterns, motivations, and goals. The more detailed you are, the better."* Another definition comes from the Buyer Persona Institute: *"Buyer personas are examples of the real buyers who influence or make decisions about the products, services or solutions you market. They are a tool that builds confidence in strategies to persuade buyers to choose you rather than a competitor or the status quo."*

The creation of buyer personas begins by understanding that customers are divided into a variety of segments. As a result, a definitive snapshot of each segment has to be discovered and articulated. As important, buyer personas need to look and feel like real people, even though they are representative of customer segments. The key to buyer persona creation is doing the research to identify their key characteristics. The deeper you dig into your customers, the better picture starts to develop. Don't worry about getting too granular in building buyer personas. It is better to have too much information than too little. There is no hard and fast rule about how many buyer personas to create, but three to five personas should cover the customer landscape. A user-friendly tool to guide the buyer persona process is Personapp (personapp.io/)

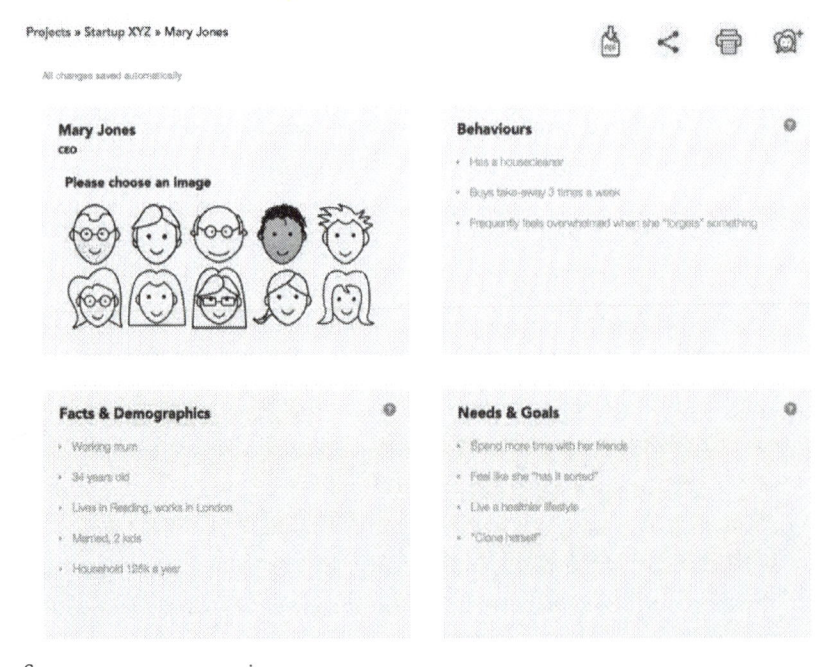

Source: www.personapp.io

Let's get going with buyer persona creation.

1. Talk to your customers, even if you don't have that many right now. Ideally, there are customers who like your product, which means they should provide good insight. (Note: I'm always puzzled why startups are reluctant to talk with their customers given that they are happy to be engaged.) You want to talk to a variety of customers - large and small, long-time and new, enthusiastic and reserved, and both happy and dissatisfied. This provides a broad customer snapshot. Do not be troubled by customers who have issues or complaints about your product; they often provide the most valuable insight and ideas.

- Be clear about your objectives. Tell people the exercise is about getting information to improve your product and the customer experience; it is not about sales. This will stop people from being defensive or thinking there are ulterior motives. As well, disclose how much time is needed. Asking for 15 to 20 minutes will seem as do-able, although many customers will want to talk longer.

- Courage: It is the adage "Don't ask, don't get". To do interviews, you need to ask people to participate. The worst thing they can say is "no" or "I'm not interested". That said, most people will agree to an interview. In my experience, customers are happy when a startup is interested in their thoughts and ideas. It suggests a startup values its customers for more than giving them money on one-time or regular basis.

It is also essential to talk to potential customers or people who decided not to do business with you. For customers thinking about buying your product, you can get insight into their needs and buying behaviour. Customers who decided not to make a purchase can tell you what failed to work for them. As much as this can be disheartening, there are lessons to be learned from failure. Maybe your product was missing key features, maybe it was too expensive, or the competition was better. This insight will help you make improvements to your business and the product.

2. Social media

Keeping a close eye on social media is a good way to get insight into what customers (and those of your rivals) are thinking, asking and doing. You can discover their interests and needs, and the things that excite or frustrate them. It can help to identify topics and themes that can be integrated into your storytelling process. An important part of capitalizing on the value of social media is tapping into the knowledge and expertise of social media and community managers, who are engaging with customers on a regular basis. Often, they have real-time insight into what is happening with customers and the marketplace. Some of the ways to leverage social media include:
- Establishing keywords that include your brand and products, and those of your rivals
- Creating a list of influencers – people who play a key part in how people think about your products, competitors and industry. This could include evangelists, buyers, analysts and the media.
- Looking for questions that a customer may have when doing research or considering a purchase.

3. Employees

Everyone from sales and marketing to customer service

and account managers - have lots of information about your customers. I have always found that customer service reps and account managers have an excellent and often untapped understanding into customers because they operate on the front lines every day. They are the people who hear first-hand about customers' problems, needs and, hopefully, things that make them happy.

4. Data

A key part of customer personas is data, which provides in-depth quantitative information. One of the best tools to access data to gain more insight about customers is Google Analytics. If you turn on the Audience feature, it tracks demographic information such as age, gender, interests, geographic location, devices used and behaviour.

What questions should be asked to create buyer personas?

- Who purchases your product?
- What are their points of pain and needs?
- How do they discover there are products in the market?
- How do you solve a buyer's problems or needs?
- What is a buyer's role in the company? (e.g. researcher, influencer, decision maker)
- What are the buyer's biggest challenges and fears?
- How does the buyer define success in the workplace?
- What are the buyer's most common hurdles to purchases?
- How does the buyer like to communicate?

After this information is collected and analyzed, you can start to create buyer personas, which includes the following ingredients:

- Name
- Job title
- Age
- Education
- Industry
- Experience
- Responsibilities
- Are they an influencer, decision maker or buyer?
- Goals
- Challenges
- Fears
- Points of pain
- Where do they get their information – blogs, publications, etc.?
- How they can they look like heroes? What does success look like?
- What are the decision-making factors - price, customer service and usability?
- How do they like interacting with sellers – email, telephone, in-person?

To create a buyer persona, this template addresses the key areas:

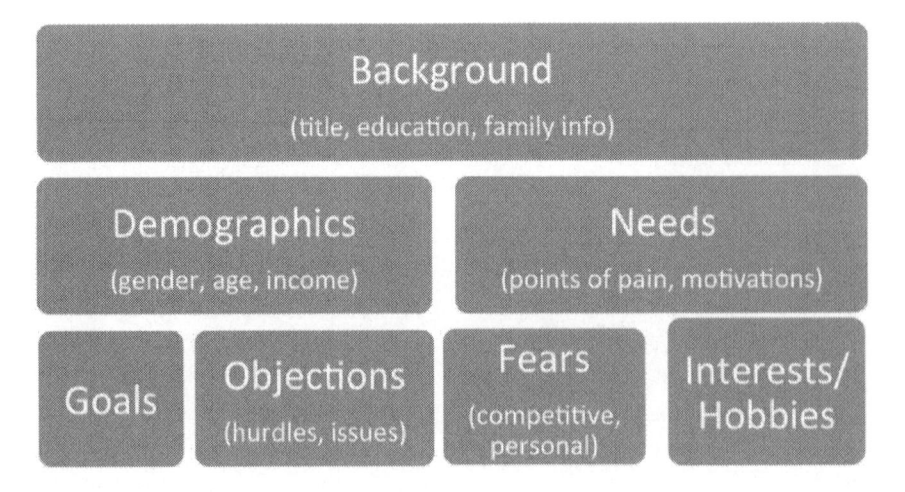

Background
(title, education, family info)

Demographics
(gender, age, income)

Needs
(points of pain, motivations)

Goals

Objections
(hurdles, issues)

Fears
(competitive, personal)

Interests/Hobbies

Here is what a buyer persona could look like:
Salima
- 35-years-old
- Director, Marketing
- B. Commerce
- Responsible for establishing marketing strategy and tactical implementation for a startup's digital and off-line activities, including content marketing and social media
- Goals: Brand awareness, leads
- Fears: A lack of ROI, a competitive landscape
- Needs: User-friendly products and services that can be quickly embraced to drive ROI
- Success: The company gains more traction to drive leads and sales

It is also important to make sure buyer personas are visible to everyone involved in marketing, sales and customer service. Here is a creative way that MailChimp uses posters to keep its buyer personas in the spotlight.

Source: http://blog.mailchimp.com/new-mailchimp-user-persona-research/

KEY TAKEAWAY:

Consumers come in different shapes and sizes. Target audiences and buyer personas consist of people who have slightly different needs and interests.

"In marketing school, you're taught the four P's: price, product, promotion and place. But these have to do with what your selling, not who you're selling to. Customer personas help you figure out who's on the other side. A customer persona is something that everyone in the company needs to understand so they can rally behind the product."
- Randy Frisch, chief operating officer, Uberflip.

KEY QUESTIONS:

1. Who are the different customers you want to target?

2. How are their needs and goals different and/or similar?

3. How do you break down the different types of customers?

4. What are the different ways you can gain insight about customers?

5. How do you ensure everyone understands customers are unique?

EXERCISE

Use a "funnel" approach to identify the people who could purchase your product. Start with a broad group (e.g. women between 25-to-44-years old). Then, split this group into sub-groups (e.g. women who are single, women who are married with children, etc.). Next, write down details about each sub-group (e.g. age, education, job titles, goals)

CHAPTER EIGHT

Talking to Your Customers

"You'll learn more in a day talking to customers than a week of brainstorming, a month of watching competitors, or a year of market research."

- Aaron Levie, CEO, Box.com

Story-driven marketing is a two-sided coin. Startups tell stories consumed by target audiences. That is a pretty simple proposition, right? But here's the thing: effective storytelling happens by having insight into your audience. What stories do they like to hear? What stories get them excited, curious, etc.? What is the trick to knowing what your audiences want? That's easy: talk to them.

This includes getting more information about their customers – something some companies think they can't or will not do because why talk to people who have already bought your product. But not talking with customers is a recipe for failure. No matter how good your idea or product, it is difficult to meet their needs and interests if you don't know your customers. Some startups may discover their product does not address what customers really need or want. Or they may find the way that early customers are actually using their product is not the way a company thought it would be used. I had a startup client, for example, that had its mobile app enthusiastically embraced as a user-friendly tool for internal communications. The app, however, was designed to drive awareness of corporate social responsibility and wellness programs. Once the startup realized how the app was being used, it switched gears and began to see more sales traction.

Stuart MacDonald, a business advisor, says startups have little money for research so they have to make educated guesses about their customers - their needs, goals, interests, buying habits, etc. A key consideration, he advises, is putting yourself in the shoes of your customers to think about their problems and how your product can resonate with them. "Even though you won't necessarily get it right, there is huge value in the act of thinking about who that prospective customer is and what is going on with them. You need to make a decision about customer profiles. Will you get it 100% right? No. For an early stage company, some of it will be a guess and a supposition. Even though a startup will not get it 100% right, they will be further ahead by virtue of having a stake in the ground."

There are many ways to talk to customers. It could be done using surveys, telephone calls, face-to-face interviews, attending conferences, or using focus groups. And here is a key consideration: customers welcome the opportunity to be engaged. To them, it means a company wants ideas and feedback as opposed to being forgotten after a purchase is made. It is important to talk with a mix of customers - customers who love your product, customers who are satisfied, and customers who are unhappy. As Bill Gates put it: "Your most unhappy customers are your greatest source of learning".

How do companies kick off the process of talking to customers? That's simple: you ask them. I told you it was simple. Here is how you do it:

1. Establish your needs and goals. What do you want to learn from talking to customers? Is it ideas for new features? Are you looking to improve the overall experience? Do you want honest feedback?

2. Identify the customers you want to target. It could be all your customers, customers who have been around for more than a year, recent customers, or customers who stopped using your product. This plays a key role about the insight being sought.

3. Create a list of questions to get the required information. To make them easy to answer, the questions should be focused and succinct. To get more insight, stay away from simple or yes/no questions.

4. Reach out to customers. This could be done using email where you ask to have a conversation. At this point, there are several options:

- To do an interview, it means sending a note explaining your goals and how you would like 15 to 20 minutes of their time to get their ideas and feedback. Then, it is a matter of being organized to arrange meetings. Tools such as Doodle, ScheduleOnce or Meet-o-Matic make it easy to create appointments to fit the schedules of multiple people.
- Surveys are also another way to communicate with customers. They are not as time-consuming but less personal. Customers are sent an email with your goals, along with a link to an online survey using tools such as SurveyMonkey or Typeform. I would suggest asking a maximum of 10 questions.

1. After someone does an interview or completes a survey, send an email thanking them for their time. You could even offer a thank you gift (e.g. gift card)

2. Aggregate the information – go through interview notes and survey answers to highlight common themes, ideas and suggestions.

3. Create a document that features actionable strategic and tactical items.

4. Explore how the interview materials can be used to create white papers, blog posts, case studies, etc.

There are, of course, many other ways to talk with customers. Steli Efti, co-founder with Close.io, says calling new customers to thank them for their business can provide opportunities to meet in person or do a phone call. Startups can also do informal customer meet-ups, host user-groups, or attend conferences.

An example of a company that really embraced the concept of talking to customers is Groove. To get a better idea about how its customers use its online ticket system to provide customer support, Groove CEO Alex Turnbull talked to 500 customers over a four-week period - an exercise that took more than 100 hours of calls. Turnbull described the process as "mind-blowingly valuable....It has changed our product, our business and the way we think. It's certainly been responsible for any growth we've had......You don't have to go on a mission to talk to every single customer. But reach out to a handful today. You might learn something that will change your business."

CASE STUDY: TALKING TO CUSTOMERS

FRESHBOOKS cloud accounting   Perhaps one of the most creative approaches to talking to customers was done by Freshbooks, an online invoicing service, whose senior executives went on a 12-day road trip in a rented RV as they travelled to two conferences: The Future of Web Apps in Miami, and the South by Southwest Interactive Festival (SXSW) in Austin, Tex. Along the way, Michael McDerment, Saul Colt and Sunir Shah stopped in different cities to have breakfast, lunch and dinner with their customers.

The "Roadburn" trip allowed Freshbooks to meet with more than 100 customers in 10 cities with stops in Miami, West Palm Beach, Orlando, Jacksonville, Tallahassee, Pensacola, Mobile,

> New Orleans, Houston, and Austin. "We really believe that we're a service, not a technology," McDerment, Freshbooks' CEO and co-founder, told IT World Canada. "We want to deliver a great experience, not software. If we want to be about service, we want to break down those barriers at every opportunity we get."

Six truths about talking to customers:

1. Customers are happy to talk. Given that few startups actually talk to customers; you score points by reaching out to them. And if the CEO does the outreach, it is even more powerful. One of my client's customers was so impressed the CEO made a call, they decided to do even more business with the company.

2. If you ask for 15 to 20 minutes, you can get more time. Once a customer gets on the phone, they are not eager to hang up. In fact, they see it as a great opportunity to provide ideas and talk about their needs.

3. Customers will tell you what they like about your product and, as important, things that make them unhappy. The criticism is more valuable than "you're doing great" because it offers much-needed perspective.

4. It is an excellent business development opportunity. Nothing says we value and want your business as much as talking to customers. It gives them more encouragement to do business with you and spread the word.

5. It provides competitive insight and intelligence about how rivals are doing business better, differently or worse.

6. You get a much better picture of your customers – their interests, needs, and points of pain. The more you know, the better you can serve them and improve at selling to potential customers.

KEY TAKEAWAY:

Talking to customers makes so much sense given they can offer valuable information, intelligence and ideas.

"Talking to customers starts from the top. A founder needs to be committed. They can't just talk about it; they need to live it and practice it before they can preach it. Like anything, changing habits involves taking small steps and being consistent rather than trying to make grand changes." – Steli Efti, co-founder and CEO, Close.io

KEY QUESTIONS:

1. Why do you need to talk to customers?

2. How do you approach customers?

3. What kind of questions should you ask?

4. What do you do with feedback, criticism, etc.?

5. How does it help your company's progress?

> **EXERCISE**
>
> Have your startup's founder or CEO send an email to five to 10 customers to see if they would invest 15 minutes of their time to provide ideas and feedback that would improve how you do business. Focus on what they like about your product and how you could make things better. As well, ask how you can support their growth.

Worksheet: Talking to Customers

Determine what you want from talking to customers • Ideas for new features • Improve the product experience • Honest feedback • Competitive intelligence
Identify target audiences • All your customers • Long-time customers • New customers (e.g. < one year) • Potential customers • Customers who picked a rival
Create a list of questions • Succinct and clear • At most, 5 to 10 questions
Reach out to customers via email • Explain goals. How much time you need • Make it easy to book interview slots (Doodle, ScheduleOnce, etc.) • Offer an option to provide feedback via email
Aggregate information • Review interview notes and email feedback • Identify common themes, ideas, feedback and criticisms • Create a report featuring actionable strategic and tactical items • Explore how information can be used to create content - e.g. white papers, blog posts, case studies.

CHAPTER NINE
Creating a Storytelling/Marketing Strategy

"We have a strategic plan. It's called doing things"
- Herb Kelleher, founder, Southwest Airlines

Creating stories that engage, educate and entertain is gratifying but a large part of storytelling success hinges on attracting the right audiences at the right time (aka Marketing 101). After all, there is not much satisfaction in telling a good story but have no one listening. Before a startup can successfully create stories, there are three key strategic questions to ask:

1. Why do you want to do marketing?

2. What are your goals and objectives?

3. What kind of marketing will happen?

The first question is obvious, but it has to be asked because marketing is a multi-faceted creature that involves different needs, goals and motivations. Some startups want to do marketing because their product has traction, so there are opportunities to accelerate growth. Some startups are scrambling to deal with competition so they are driven more by defense than offense. Some startups want to leverage marketing to raise capital. And some startups believe the time is right for marketing but have little idea about what is involved.

The foundation for a good marketing strategy starts with being honest on the "why". It sets the stage for the key pillars to be defined. It forces entrepreneurs to get a better handle about their marketing and business needs. Without answering "why", it is easy for a startup's marketing to fall short of expectations. Marketing without defined goals can go astray, leading to disappointment, frustration and little return on investment.

So, rule #1 is: Be clear on why marketing is being embraced.

The second question - what you do want to get from marketing? - is important so objectives and metrics are established, preferably right out of the gate. It makes no sense to do marketing for the sake of marketing; otherwise marketing is a waste of time. A startup needs well-articulated goals to grow the business. It could be brand awareness to drive more leads and sales, better articulation of its unique value propositions and benefits to establish a competitive differentiation, or creating a better story and collateral to raise capital.

Here is how one of my clients mapped out its marketing goals:

1. Drive more leads and sales, particularly from non-referral sources. This includes merchants currently using traditional direct marketing, or companies currently not using cost-per-aequisition advertising.

2. Establish the company as a distinctive player within the affiliate marketing sector so it can be seen as the most results-driven player.

3. A higher brand profile and awareness to drive more attention from merchants, partners and affiliates.

4. Clear messaging that makes it easy to tell key stakeholders what the company does and the value it delivers.

5. Clarity about core competencies, benefits, features and target audiences.

6. Defining the service as a product. This includes being more clear about the different services offered to advertisers.

If you review the list, these are straightforward goals. They gave the company a clear sense of where it wanted to go. Once these goals were established, it was easier to determine what needed to happen and who needed to be targeted.

In some respects, the "why marketing" and "what goals" questions come from the same philosophical camp as Simon Sinek's *Golden Circle*, which is a key part of his popular book *"Start With Why"* - www.startwithwhy.com. At the core of the Golden Circle is "why", which is a company's core belief and why it exists. "How" is how the business meets that core belief, while "What" are the things that a company does to drive the business forward to meet its beliefs.

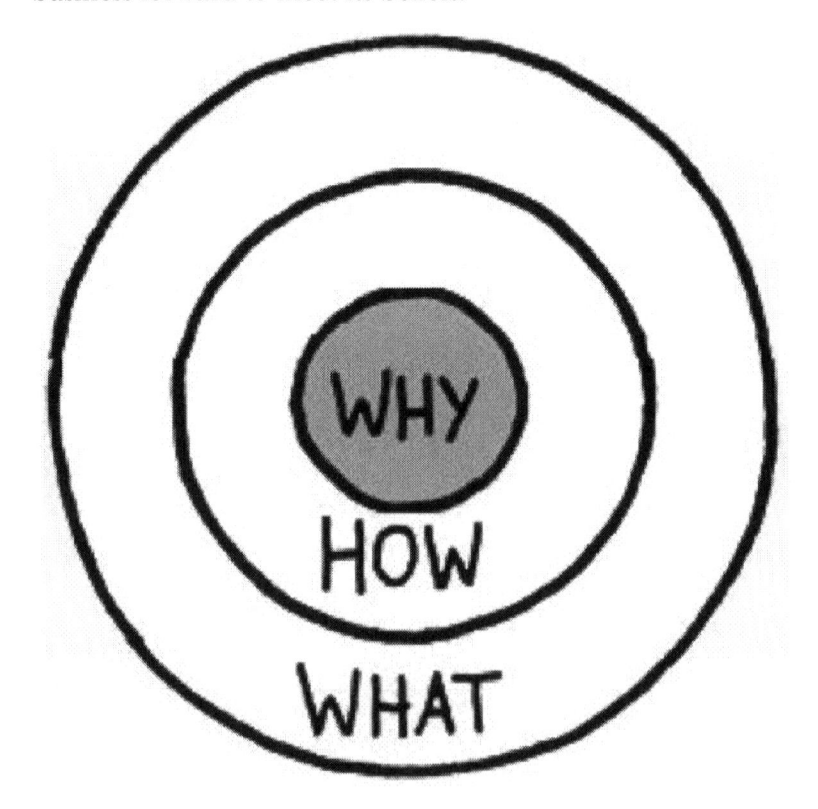

Source: www.startupwithwhy.com

To explain how the Golden Circle works, Sinek uses Apple as an example. One of the reasons, he says, for Apple's success is how it is driven by why rather than what. Here is how

Sinek's articulates it: "Everything we (Apple) do, we believe in challenging the status quo. We believe in thinking differently. The way we challenge the status quo is by making our products beautifully designed, simple to use and user-friendly. And we happen to make great computers. Wanna buy one?"

After a startup's "why" and the "goals" are articulated, the next strategic steps are focused on these key elements:

1. Who should hear our stories?
2. Where and how do we find these people?
3. What kind of stories do they like to hear?
4. How can we tell if our stories are working?

Asking these questions is a critical exercise because a story's appeal does not mean much if it is not delivered to the right people at the right time in the right places. A mistake made by many startups is not doing enough or, for that matter, any strategic planning at all. Far too often, "planning" is a seat of the pants process in which decisions are made based on intuition, gut feeling or guesses.

For storytelling to work, there has to be a well-defined plan with clear goals - be it brand awareness, media coverage, Web-site traffic, partnerships, leads or sales. It means being crystal clear about what needs to be achieved, and the benchmarks and metrics to measure progress and success. A marketing strategy sets the stage for stories to be created and told in certain ways at certain times. It provides structure to the marketing a startup will do in the short, medium and long term. An important element in creating a marketing strategy is not only identifying the opportunities but also ranking them to align with your budget and resources (people, time). It is about driving return on investment. Out of the many available options, a startup has to decide where it will get bang for the buck. When you only have so many bullets, you need to be prudent about when and how to use them. In many respects, the marketing mix hinges on deciding where your stories will make the biggest impact. As Groove CEO Alex Turnbull says, "what efforts would be the highest and best use of every team member's time?"

One of the challenges in deciding where to focus is the number of options. It is like eating at a Denny's restaurant. The menu is so large, it can be difficult to make a decision about what to order. (This is probably why most people order the "Grand Slam" for breakfast!) The same challenges face startups when the "menu" can include:

- Websites
- Social media
- Videos
- White papers
- Traditional media (newspapers, radio, TV)
- Case studies
- One-pagers (aka sales sheets)
- Infographics
- Sales decks
- Podcasts
- Conferences (speaking, attending, sponsoring)
- Advertising (AdWords, Facebook, banner ads, etc.)

In an ideal world, startups tell their stories everywhere to maximize exposure. The reality, however, is most startups have limited marketing budgets so it is important to align resources (people, money) with the most effective channels. It's a focused rather than a shotgun approach.

"Startup marketing is similar to the whole startup philosophy in general," says Neil Bhapkar, chief marketing officer with FlightNetwork. "You have a product but you're constrained by resources, budget and knowledge. The key to startup marketing is having a laser focus because you can't do everything. Instead, you have to prioritize on one or two areas that will be realistic based on the team, resources, budget and cash flow."

The insight into establishing priorities will come from talking to potential and existing customers about their needs and the buying process. Hopefully, they tell you where they get information about the market in which you play. If, for example, potential customers use Twitter to do research and ask questions about the products that you are selling, it is a no-brainer to have an active presence on Twitter. On the other hand, it probably makes little sense for a B2B startup to invest a lot of time and effort on Facebook, unless it is doing something unique or creative.

Stuart MacDonald, a business advisor, says marketing involves trial and error. "It is called a marketing mix for a reason," he says. "People talk about the marketing mix of price, product, place and promotion. It is those four P's that cause a sale to happen. Even in the promotion piece, which is what non-marketers mean by marketing, there is a mix. There are lots of different things you can do and you're not going to find one silver bullet to get it all done, in one fell swoop. You run a lot of tests, look at the results and do more of the things going well, and less of the things not going well."

A good approach to establishing marketing priorities is a technique created by Justin Wilcox, who blogs about marketing at CustomerDevLabs.com, called "The SPA treatment". Wilcox uses SPA to roughly identify the customers he wants to interview, but it can be "hacked" to determine marketing priorities. The "S" stands for "size" – the number of potential customers in the market. "P" stands for the likelihood a customer will pay, while "A" stands for "access" – how easy a customer can be accessed and converted into a customer. SPA is used to rank potential customers against the three parameters. Here is how Wilcox ranked three potential target audiences for an app that would help people get to meetings on time. A "3" indicates a segment having the most potential. (Note: The video can be seen here: bit.ly/1xPC8AZ)

Potential Client	Size	Pay	Access
Real Estate Agent	2	2	2
College Freshman	3	1	1
Techies with ADD	2	3	3

The SPA Treatment can be used to create marketing priorities. Here is how it would work for a high-tech snow shovel. (Clearly, a product that would work in Canada!) In this example, homeowners would have the most interest in our high-tech snow shovel, while home renters would rank second.

Potential Client	Size	Pay	Access
Homeowners	3	3	3
Home Renters	2	2	2
Gadget Lovers	2	2	1

The need to be strategically flexible, agile and opportunistic.

Last, but not least, startups need to be flexible, agile and opportunistic. Sometimes, you have time to plan for opportunities; sometimes, they suddenly emerge. The reality is change is constant: change in your product, customers, technology, marketplace, competitors and the economic landscape. It means iterating, being open to shifts and making real-time strategic and tactical adjustments. Experimentation is also important, as well as an ability to quickly scale when things are working.

KEY TAKEAWAY:

An important part of creating an effective marketing strategy is determining what you want to achieve with the resources (people, money) to make it happen, and then setting priorities.

"The essence of strategy is choosing what not to do." - Michael Porter, economist, researcher and author.

KEY QUESTIONS:

1. Why do marketing?

2. What are your goals and objectives?

3. Who are your target audiences?

4. What are the available resources (time, money, people?)

5. How do you set priorities (aka activities that offer bang for the buck)?

> **EXERCISE**
> List all the potential marketing options that could be tapped (include any channel that would make sense). Then, rank each option based on its effectiveness to get potential customers into the sales funnel.

Marketing Strategy Worksheet

To help frame discussions about a marketing strategy, this worksheet has a list of the key questions to ask about your motivations, product, customers and competitors:

Why marketing?
• What are your motivations, interests and needs?
Goals
• What are your objectives?   • What do you want to achieve?   • What does success look like?
Product
• What products do you sell?   • What makes your product unique?   • How is it priced?   • How is it sold?
Target Audiences
• Who are the key stakeholders?   • Who's the ideal customer?   • Who are your best customers?
Buyer Personas
• Demographics – background, education, titles, needs, challenges, goals

Selling
- How do you pursue business?
- How do customers find you?
- Where do customers get information about products in the market?
- How long is the sales cycle?
- Why do customers buy your products?
- What keeps potential customers from buying your product?
- What marketing or sales collateral could improve the sales funnel?

The Market
- How big is the market?
- How fast is the market growing?
- What's driving growth?
- How much competition is there?
- What are the barriers to entry?

Competitive Landscape
- Who are the direct competitors?
- What are they doing well?
- Who are the indirect rivals? What keeps them in the market? (e.g. Freshbooks vs. Quicken)
- Who are the most interesting players? What are the biggest opportunities in the next 6 to 12 months?

Marketing activity (current)
- What's your current marketing activity?
- What marketing collateral is being used?
- What is working?

CHAPTER TEN

Defining and Measuring Storytelling Success

"80% of success is showing up"
- Woody Allen.

Storytelling is important but it is easy to spin your wheels without goals and measuring how well your stories are performing. Is anyone engaging with your stories? Are they connecting with target audiences? Are they successful in getting people to take actions: visit the Website, watch videos, download white papers, ask for demos, make purchases, etc.? If your stories are not working, they are, frankly, a waste of time and resources. Measuring performance offers the insight to refresh the stories being told, change the channels used, or reallocate resources.

Success is measured in different ways. For some startups, it is about sales or leads. For others, it can be pageviews, downloads or new users. Whatever the metrics, it is important to define what success looks like so everyone knows the goals being pursued. Here are some different approaches:

1. Analytics, which provide a wealth of information to guide strategic and tactical decisions. This information shows what stories are working and what stories are failing to resonate. To get the most value from analytics, it is important to create a list of metrics to benchmark success. A "success list" could include:

- Visits (traffic)
- New versus repeat visitors
- Page views
- Pages per visit
- The 5 or 10 most popular pages
- Time on site
- People who completed an action: made a purchase, downloaded content, filled out a form, requested for a demo, etc.
- People who visited another page
- Bounce rate (the number of people who visited on page before leaving)

- What Websites that delivered traffic to you
- Search engines used – e.g. Google, Yahoo and Bing.
- Visits from desktop computers and mobile devices

Bryan McCaw, founder of WineAlign.com, says the biggest value provided by analytics is how it keeps entrepreneurs sane. "Fundamentally, it is about being able to measure traffic to your Website and looking for trends. Looking for trends keeps you sane; otherwise you are operating in a vacuum. If you see growth month over month, it gives you a sense that things are moving in the right direction and reasons to keep on going."

There are many analytical tools to drill much deeper in the numbers. They include:

- Google Analytics: The world's most popular Web analytics tool, Google Analytics provides a free version with lots of features, along with a premium service.

- Chartbeat delivers real-time information about traffic using a user-friendly interface that makes it easy to see what's happening.

- Woopra is a leading real-time web analytics and targeted customer engagement service.

- Clicky: A free and low-cost service to track and analyze Website traffic

- Quill Engage, which offers analytics reports in a user-friendly way that anyone can understand (quillengage.narrativescience.com/)

- Visual.ly's Google Analytics report: an infographic-like reporting tool (https://create.visual.ly/graphic/google-analytics)

Note: We are lightly touching the Web analytics market. For more insight, here are some good resources:

- Google Analytics blog - http://analytics.blogspot.ca/
- Jonathan Mendez: http://bit.ly/1xVLaNf
- Avinash Kaushik: http://www.kaushik.net/
- Danny Sullivan: http://selnd.com/1IB2IPY
- Rand Fishkin: http://moz.com/rand/

2. Surveys are a good way to gain insight from customers. Of course, there are best practices and tricks to create effective surveys. At the top of the list is making sure they are user-friendly. You want to make a survey appear so easy that it requires little effort to complete it. We have all come across surveys - even from companies we like - that take so much time and effort that they are quickly abandoned.

Here are the steps to create high-response surveys:

1. Determine the information or insight you want to collect. A focused approach is the most effective way to get responses.
2. Create a list of questions. Five to 10 questions is ideal because it generates solid information without asking people to do too much work. I have also seen effective one-question surveys that include a comment box.
3. Identify the target audience. It could be all your customers, recent customers, customers who use a free service, etc. It depends on the information to be collected.
4. Send an email that includes a short introduction about

the survey's purpose and how much time it will take, along with a link to the survey. At this point, you can offer an incentive to do the survey.
5. When someone completes the survey, send a thank you email.
6. If someone does not participate in the survey, follow up with another invitation in a week.
7. Aggregate the survey results, including participation rates, to analyze the information that has been collected.
8. Create a report that highlights the key findings, including actionable insight to make strategic and tactical changes.

At the end of the day, surveys are "Trojan Horses". While you want many people engaged, what you really want are people who love what you are doing…and dislike what you are doing. The value comes from the extremes. The people who love you will have no problem talking about how your product rocks the house. On the flip side, people who are not fans will deliver insight into how your product fails to meet their needs. The extremes are invaluable because they offer different perspectives. Here are some online tools (free and paid) that make it easy to create and distribute surveys:

- SurveyMonkey (surveymonkey.com)
- Poll Daddy (polldaddy.com)
- Fluid Surveys (fluidsurveys.com/)
- Zoomerang (zoomerang.com)
- Typeform (typeform.com)
- Google Forms (google.ca/forms/about/)
- Qualaroo (qualaroo.com)

3. Social media: To get a real-time sense of how well your stories are working, watch what is happening on social media.

How many people are talking about your stories: posting links on Twitter, Facebook, LinkedIn and Pinterest, linking to them in blog posts, leaving blog comments, watching videos, or viewing or downloading your presentations on Slideshare? While it takes legwork (having user-friendly social media monitoring and analytics tools is a good idea), social media delivers real-time insight and, as important, feedback. Here is how to tap into the power of social media to measure the success of your efforts:

1. Identify keywords to monitor – your brand, products, market, and competitors. Some of the tools to monitor social media activity include TweetDeck, Hootsuite, Twitter search and Buzzsumo.
2. When you see a keyword mentioned, drill down into the person behind it to get more information about what they do and how much influence they may have.
3. Look for referral traffic from social media networks. Your Website analytics tools (e.g. Google Analytics) will provide details on where traffic is coming from.

There are literally thousands of online tools to monitor, track, manage and publish on social media. Here is a list of some of the most popular:

- HootSuite (hootsuite.com)
- Sysomos (sysomos.com)
- Buzzsumo (buzzsumo.com)
- TweetDeck (tweetdeck.com)
- Social Mention (socialmention.com)
- Ice Rocket (icerocket.com)
- Topsy (topsy.com)

4. Talking to your customers: Want to really know how you are doing? Ask the people using your product. It's that simple. And here's the *remarkable* thing: most customers are happy to talk and they are willing to provide honest feedback that will delight, surprise, disappoint or alarm you. In other words, they will provide a real-world litmus test offering a much-needed dose of reality. There are many ways to talk with customers. You can invite them to dinner, coffee, special events or conferences. You can ask if they would be interested in doing a case study. Even when a case study candidate does not pan out, you usually get valuable feedback. Stuart MacDonald, a business advisor who has worked with many startups, says spending time with customers in informal and formal setting is huge. "You can get a live focus group by spending time with these folks. Make it a point to talk with people and understand what is going on with them, understand why they gravitated to you, and what you are doing well. It is important to spend the time to learn from them." (Note: In Chapter 8, there is more information and guidance on how to talk to customers.)

5. Engage your employees: Another way to get the "scoop" about your company's performance is asking the people who spend a lot of time talking with customers: customer service representatives and account managers. While you are marketing or selling, your employees are dealing with customers' problems and criticism, as well as fielding feedback and ideas. There is a wealth of information about everything they hear from customers. To get this information, you could create a digital feedback "box". Holding a town hall meeting is another way to learn what customers are saying, as well as getting employees involved and engaged in driving how the business operates.

Measuring the success of storytelling is a multi-faceted creature because success means different things to different companies. What may be successful storytelling for one company may not meet the goals of another. Regardless of how success is measured, the most important consideration is establishing performance benchmarks. They provide guidance on how far you have come and how well you are doing. They allow people to get excited and maintain their efforts, or offer an important feedback loop that shows how strategies or tactics need to be tweaked or overhauled.

KEY TAKEAWAY:
There are many ways to define and measure success. Not all of them have to do with numbers or data; some of it is how happy you make the customer.

"If at first you don't succeed, try, try again. Then quit. No use being a damn fool about it." - W.C. Fields.

KEY QUESTIONS:
1. How do you define success qualitatively and quantitatively?

2. What do you want to specifically measure?

3. How will you measure it and how often?

4. How do you analyze success or failure?

5. What are the actionable insights from measuring success?

EXERCISE

Create a free account on Google Analytics to see how your Website is performing. Identify the most important metrics – e.g. pageviews, unique visitors, time on site, referrals. Then, check these metrics every day to identify trends. As well, use Quill Engage (quillengage.narrativescience.com/) to get weekly reports.

CHAPTER 11

Who Gets To Tell Stories?

"Great stories happen to those who can tell them."
- **Ira Glass**

Most startups have a small number of employees, particularly startups that have embraced the lean approach advocated by author and Silicon Valley entrepreneur Eric Ries. With few voices, it makes sense to adopt a collective approach to storytelling that involves everyone (employees, investors, advisors, partners, etc.). One of the challenges is making sure they read from the "same page in the hymn book" when telling the corporate story. Getting everyone to be a startup storyteller is a powerful way to make people see themselves as key players on the road to success, rather than being cogs in the machine.

Let's look at the different kinds of startup storytellers:

Founders

As the visionaries, business leaders and, often, the biggest investors, founders play a huge role in storytelling. In many cases, they are the lead storyteller because they are so vested in their startup's creation and growth. The problem is many startup founders are not natural storytellers so, like everyone else, they need to learn how to deliver compelling narratives that reflect a startup's raison d'être as much as its vision and mission. They need to know the story inside out and understand how to deliver it in different ways to different audiences.

A big storytelling hurdle for founders is recognizing the role they need to play, even when there are other employees with better storytelling skills. More than anyone, a founder has credibility and an authentic story to deliver given they have been involved since the beginning. This makes it easier for founders to develop a narrative that contains the key elements of good storytelling: optimism, drama, challenges and, hopefully, success.

At the same time, the stories told by founders need to evolve. The story conveyed to friends and family after a startup is launched is different from the story told to potential employees and investors. And the story changes as a startup's product is developed, marketing and sales people are hired, customers are attracted, investors arrive, or new competitors enter the market. For a founder, it means their storytelling has to be agile and opportunistic. They need to understand that stories are delivered in different ways to different audiences (media, investors, employees, partners, etc.) seeking different things.

Michael McDerment, co-founder and chief executive with Freshbooks, said he struggled with storytelling because he wanted to constantly tell it differently, rather than repeating the same story over and over again. "I came to realize a big part of your job as a startup CEO is you are the chief story re-teller," he says. "A big part of my job is telling the story and telling it consistently. I used to get tired of my own story when I was telling it because I wanted to make it new and different. But I forgot the audience was hearing it for the first time. Instead of changing it up for their benefit, the best-polished story is one you repeat. I struggled with that for a long time but that is part of my role and job description. Now, I can tell the story in 10 seconds, 30 seconds, five minutes or 90 minutes. I think there is another thing: understanding that you need to communicate your story in different lengths effectively, and that comes with practice. That is an important concept."

Storytelling 101 for Founders

1. Create a story or several versions of a story, and then practice until you have it down cold. Telling the story frequently makes it easier to see what works and what needs improvement. Like a comedian who culls jokes that fail to generate laughs, startup founders

need to hone their story to make it more effective and compelling. Aside from practice, storytelling gets better through media training (aka how to talk to reporters and bloggers), and/or public speaking training.

2. Look for opportunities to tell your story. It could be conferences, demos, media interviews, coffee meetings, or presentations to employees, investors, analysts or partners. The more a story is told, the better it gets. It is not only the content but the delivery and the reaction it generates.

3. Embrace the role as a startup's chief storyteller. If it is a role that you enjoy, have fun with it. If you are not a natural storyteller, keep telling stories until it starts to flow better, and/or seek help to turn yourself into a decent, if not good, storyteller. There are many founders who initially struggled with being public storytellers before growing into the role. It may not be something they like to do but it is something they have to do.

Employees

Every employee needs to be a powerful storyteller and brand advocate. Employees should effectively be able to communicate what the startup does, the product's value, and who should be using it. They should be able to tell a story in different situations - customer support calls, sales meetings, meet-ups, conferences, etc. If employees can tell your story, you have an engaged army to spread the word in many places.

How can startups arm employees with the story?

1. Begin by having well articulated messaging so everyone can read off the same page. Strong messaging offers consistency across the board and gives employees a rock-solid reference point so they are always on point.

2. Get your employees involved in the storytelling process. Storytelling is not the domain of the executive suite or the marketing department. It is not something that suddenly comes down from above. Good storytelling happens when many people are involved in how things are shaped. It happens during town hall meetings, informal brainstorming sessions, surveys, or even something as "old school" as a suggestion box. This makes it easier for ideas to emerge. One of the best ways to transform employees into storytellers is letting them write for the corporate blog. This generates good content and provides different perspectives than the founder or someone in marketing. And, who knows, it may be a way to discover a blogging star!

3. For startups with enough resources, a community or social media manager can also be a huge storytelling asset. With a solid public profile, community and social media managers have many opportunities to tell stories that engage target audiences. Some of them happen spontaneously (e.g. chatting on Twitter, Facebook), while others are more structured such as speaking at conferences and meet-ups.

Customers

In many respects, a startup's best storytellers are their customers. These are people who have embraced a startup's product. Hopefully, they are happy to talk about a startup - be it word of mouth, blog posts or via social media. As much as startups rely on marketing and sales to drive the sales funnel, customers are a key part of the mix. For a startup with a limited marketing budget, it is a huge advantage to have customers become marketers and storytellers.

There are two sides to turning customers into storytellers. One, startups need to make them part of the storytelling machine. It is important that customers take a starring role in how a startup puts the spotlight on its business. This achieves two objectives: it makes the customer realize their business is valued, and shows potential customers there are good things happening. Some of the ways to celebrate the customer include case studies, videos, blog posts and newsletters. These are places where a customer's stories (how the product improved how they did business) can be thrust into the spotlight.

The other side of the storytelling coin is encouraging customers to tell their own stories. The UPS Store, for example, launched a campaign that encouraged small business owners to tell their stories on Twitter and Instagram using the hashtag #ViaStories. The UPS Store shared and promoted these stories on viastories.theupsstore.com, as well as through social media. Another example is Shopify, which asked its customers if they would be interested in creating case studies for the Shopify blog on how they were using the company's e-commerce platform.

If you can figure out ways to encourage customers to tell stories about how they are using your product and the value being delivered, that is powerful and authentic. Sometimes, your product is so good and your community so engaged that customer storytelling naturally happens. In other cases, you may have to "seed" the market by giving customers incentives to create stories. It could be the opportunity to be featured on your Website, invitations to an event, or winning a prize. With just a little encouragement, the stories could flow.

The power of customer testimonials

"Testimonials are great persuasion engines. They are what convince those buyers who are on the proverbial "fence" to take the leap and work with you" - Ricardo Bueno

One of the easiest and most effective ways to have customers tell stories on your behalf are testimonials. At first blush, testimonials are the Rodney Dangerfield - "I don't get no respect" of the marketing world. It is easy to dismiss testimonials as canned content dutifully delivered by happy customers (and only happy customers). And while that might, in fact, be true, the reality is testimonials work. Many customers need validation or comfort before making a purchase. They want to know that their decision is not a mistake or something they will regret. In some cases, all they need to make a purchase is a sentence or two from someone who has gone before them.

So how do you get testimonials from customers? You ask them. Simple, right? Actually, you want to do some homework before asking customers to hand over glowing testimonials. For one, it is important to get comments from customers who have different needs or problems. After all, not every potential customer is exactly the same, so you need to appeal to them using different angles. As important, not every testimonial has to be over-the-top positive, although happy customers are a good thing. It is a matter of providing a variety of perspectives so there is a sense of authenticity. In asking for testimonials, you want to be transparent about why they are needed and how they will be used. It is also a good idea to give customers the opportunity to give final approval before testimonials are published. Once you get testimonials, they can be used in a variety of ways. Some startups will use them on the homepage, while others will place testimonials on a "Clients" or "About" page. Testimonials can also be used in sales decks, one-pagers and sales brochures.

KEY TAKEAWAY:
There are different types of storytellers - some of them operate using a "corporate script", while others tell their own stories based on personal experiences.

"Those who tell stories, rule society." - Plato

KEY QUESTIONS:
1. What are the different kinds of storytellers?

2. What are their storytelling skills?

3. Who gets to tell stories?

4. How do you get employees to become storytellers?

5. How can customers tell stories for you?

EXERCISE
Identify the people within your startup who have the most storytelling potential. Look at how their storytelling skills can be improved, and the opportunities for them to tell stories.

CHAPTER 12

Influencers Are Storytellers Too

"To work with influencers requires engagement and creativity from you. Once you find your influencers, you will need a plan to engage them."
- Evy Wilkins

In recent years, the influencer has attained mythical proportions. With the emergence of social media, influencers have unprecedented reach to tell your story to drive awareness and actions (aka leads and sales). There have always been influencers but with so much competition, many startups believe they need influencers to carve out an edge. Influencers come in different shapes and sizes: high-profile bloggers, reporters, analysts, industry executives, academics or consultants. The common denominator is they have strong networks and the ability to shape opinions and ideas.

For many companies, influencers are an enticing proposition because they can provide a major boost….if you can get their attention. This is not an easy task because there is, not surprisingly, competition for influencers. It means having a strategic and focused approach that includes building an in-depth dossier on each influencer - what they do, their interests (personal and professional), their social media activities, and where they can be reached (email, blogs, conferences, etc.)

"The importance of influencers is massive," said Frank Falcone, founder and CEO with Triggerfox, a startup that offers a mobile application for building and maintaining professional relationships. "As a startup, you have no brand and no one knows you from Adam. Whether you're making widgets or CRM software, there are influencers in your space who are revered, so you want their vote of confidence."

8 Things Influencers Can Do For You

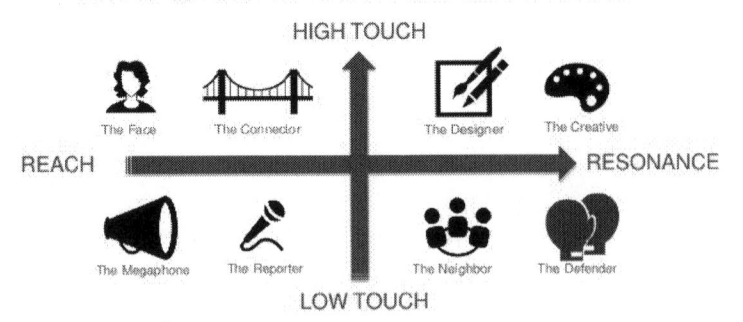

HIGH TOUCH

REACH			RESONANCE
The Face	The Connector	The Designer	The Creative
The Megaphone	The Reporter	The Neighbor	The Defender

LOW TOUCH

Source: www.tapinfluence.com

1. The Megaphone: Spread the Word to Their Audience
2. The Reporter: Cover Your Event Like a Journalist
3. The Face: Be a Spokesperson for Your Brand
4. The Connector: Introduce Your Brand on a New Social Platform
5. The Creative: Produce Creative Content for Your Brand
6. The Designer: Help Create New Product/Services for Your Brand
7. The Neighbor: Spark and Facilitate Conversations in Your Brand's Online Community
8. The Defender: Support Your Brand in Times of Crisis

How do startups win over influencers?

1. Share their content: It may sound simple but the fuel for influencers is their ability to stay influential and remain in the spotlight. A good way to nurture relationships with influencers is sharing their content such as blog posts, tweets, infographics, etc. It says you value their work so you want to amplify it. Sharing content is one of the easiest influencer tactics. By sharing an influencer's content, a startup can associate their brand with someone who has a much bigger brand.

2. Comment on blogs: For many influencers, a blog is an effective way to establish a digital footprint and put the spotlight on their ideas. For startups, commenting on an influencer's blog provides an opening to become a part of their world. A good example is entrepreneur William Mougayar, who frequently commented on the blog of Fred Wilson, a well-known venture capitalist, blogger and, yes, influencer. Mougayar became a key member of Wilson's "community" and established a personal connection. When Mougayar launched a startup, Engagio, he used Wilson's blog to get feedback. One thing led to another, and Wilson participated in Engagio's seed round.

3. Meet them: In a digital world, we sometimes forget face-to-face meetings establish powerful connections. When I was a newspaper reporter, it would take a single coffee meeting to turn a reluctant analyst into an enthusiastic and reliable source. The same goes for influencers, who are "just plain folks" despite their industry stature. The key is doing your homework to get a foothold so you can meet them. It could be a shared connection, an email or LinkedIn introduction, or approaching them at an event.

4. Ask for their advice: There is a certain amount of ego in being an influencer, as well as satisfaction in being someone whose opinion is respected. A good way to play into this emotion is asking for an influencer's feedback, ideas or advice.

5. Create content with them: Here's the thing about influencers; they are always looking to expand their footprint. And while it is good to be an influencer, it takes work to stay current and relevant. One of the ways influencers can be more effective and productive is creating content with other people, particularly if the other party does a lot of the work. But this can be a win-win scenario: the startup gets to connect and work with an influencer, while the influencer expands their content portfolio. Sure, it sounds like a tilted arrangement but both sides get what they want.

6. Be creative: When all else fails, it takes out of the box thinking to attract the attention of an influencer. A good example is Triggerfox, which offers a hand-written note service as part of mobile networking application. Frank Falcone, Triggerfox's founder and CEO, wanted to connect with a journalist, who was well-known for writing about business techniques such as hand-written notes. After finding the journalist's address, Falcone wrote a hand-written note that explained what Triggerfox did. He received a quick response because he tapped into something that established a connection. "Influencers want to know you put the effort to thoroughly research them, rather than just doing a simple Google search," Falcone said. "I did something that stood apart from the crowd and it was related to her space. You have to do the stuff that makes you stand out from the crowd and shows the influencer you have been following them."

What are the different ways to identify influencers?

There is no scientific or tried and true way to identify influencers because influencers come in different sizes and stripes. There are, however, different approaches to identifying the influencers relevant to your startup.

1. Manual: This is old-fashioned research and legwork. It involves identifying people through Web searches, reading blogs, newspapers and magazines, looking at who writes about the competition, and who is asked to speak at industry events.

2. Technology: If manual identification of influencers is the "Model T" approach, technology is a "Ferrari". Armed with an endless number of tools to use, startups can dive into the Web and social media worlds to discover people talking about their brand, products, rivals and industry. Tools such as Appinions, Buzzsumo, Influitive, FollowerWonk, TapInfluence, LinkedIn and Klout can be used to drive influencer discovery.

Once you identify influencers, create a database or spreadsheet that includes the following information:

- Name
- Title
- Organization
- Email
- Location
- Website
- What makes them an influencer?
- Interests
- Social media profiles

Having a target list of influencers is an effective tool to manage influencer relations. It provides startups with a guide on who should be monitored, whose content should be read and shared, and who they should focus on to build relationships.

CASE STUDY: ENGAGING WITH INFLUENCERS

Atomic Reach, a content marketing startup, wanted to connect with influencers, so it decided to use Twitter chats - interactive interviews done on Twitter. Atomic Reach was a relatively unknown startup but it managed to attract high-profile guests for the hour-long chat by simply asking if they were interested. It is a good example of why there is no harm in asking someone to do something. The worse they can say is "no, thanks".

Here is a Q&A with Summer Lu, a digital marketer with Atomic Reach, about how the Twitter chats operate:

1. Why did Atomic Reach decide to do Twitter chats?

We first decided to do Twitter chats for one reason: build a community around the brand. However, we soon realized we were getting much more out of it. Thought leadership, lead generation, brand advocacy, education and spotting trends are just some of the benefits that comes out of hosting a chat, and we're so proud to be part of the Twitter community.

2. What were you looking to achieve?

We started our weekly chat around the same time that Atomic Reach was created. Being a new startup in the crowded content marketing world, we were looking to gain exposure in a scalable way. Two years later, hosting weekly chats continues to be a fantastic way to break through the clutter. Along the way, we've met a lot of savvy people whom we would have not been able to connect with otherwise.

3. How do you decide on the guest to invite?

Our guests are knowledgeable and experts in their field. We like to discuss relevant topics that help content marketers improve their workflow and become their own expert in their professional lives. Whether it be about creating engaging content, growing a Facebook page or digging into audience insights, we welcome anyone who has insightful tips in the content marketing and social media worlds.

4. Is there a trick to getting high-profile guests to appear?

No tricks at all. Be genuine in your approach: ask and you shall receive. When I read a compelling article that displays a unique take or expert advice, I reach out to the author to see if they would like to be a guest on our chat.

5. Do your guests ask for anything in return? If so, what?

Our guests rarely ask for anything in return. We always appreciate the time people take to appear on our hour-long chats so we support them by promoting their content.

6. Have you found it easier to get people to appear now the chats have a track record?

It has never been hard to secure guests. People love sharing their

> knowledge with an attentive and engaging audience like ours.
>
> 7. How do you quantify the success of a chat?
>
> While we do track the impressions and reach of each chat, I base the true success of a chat by the number of new members who join the discussion. To me, new members mean our hashtag is being seen and it is intriguing enough for people to join the discussion. The greatest compliment is when we've turned a new member into a regular one.

KEY TAKEAWAY:

Influencers can have a huge impact on how people perceive your brand and product. The challenge is figuring out who is an influencer and how to engage them.

"Influencer marketing at its core is about developing real relationships to ultimately champion your influencers to market with you." – Amanda Maksymiw

KEY QUESTIONS:

1. What do you want influencers to do for you?

2. What are you going to do for them?

3. Who are the most relevant influencers for your company?

4. How do you identify and reach out to them?

5. What kind of programs will you do with influencers?

EXERCISE

Do some research to identify a small group of influencers – let's say five to 10. Then, start building relationships by following them on social media, sharing their content, and leaving comments on their blogs. Create a spreadsheet with information about these influencers.

CHAPTER 13

Setting the Stage for Media Coverage

"Build your network before you need them."
- Jeremiah Owing, partner, Altimeter Group

One of the biggest misconceptions among startups is that media coverage occurs when you really, really want it. As a result, many startups look for media and blog coverage to happen quickly if and when they have something interesting to announce. (Note: What is "interesting" to many startups is frequently not interesting to the media)

Unfortunately, it does not work that way. Sure, some startups catch lightning in a bottle (and media coverage) because their story is so compelling, unique or interesting. But most startups (and businesses, for that matter) are not that interesting, unique or newsworthy. For these startups, attracting the media spotlight means doing a lot of grunt work and preparations to set the stage for potential coverage. It is not the sexiest approach because it requires patience and a willingness to invest the necessary time and energy.

Mike Katchen, founder and CEO with Wealthsimple, said most startups are terrible at attracting media coverage because they don't understand how the game works. "Their approach is 'we are launching so they should write about us'. They send an email to whomever they will find at the Globe & Mail, TechCrunch, etc. saying 'We are launching a new app. Want to write about us?' Instead, you need to do the work for them. You need to understand that people in the press get a thousand pitches a day and 80% of their work is going through those pitches and figuring out which ones are great. If you can make the job easy, you stand out."

Like anything, timing is everything

Before getting into the mechanics of media relations, here is a big caveat: You do not want to jump the gun by seeking media attention before your product is ready for the spotlight. Startups

> with a minimal viable product or still seeking product-market fit should probably hold off on media outreach until they are ready. The problem in being too early is getting criticized, and not having another shot to make a good impression. The classic case of a startup that jumped the gun was Flock, which released an alpha version of its much-hyped Web browser in 2008. The product was universally panned, and Flock quickly faded into the background.

How does media relations work?

To be honest, there is a lot of unglamorous blocking and tackling. Long before a startup attempts to reach out to reporters or bloggers, a lot of work happens behind the scenes.

It begins with creating a target list of the reporters and bloggers that you want to cover your startup. These lists are crafted over time and built through research and networking. They anchor your media relations and public relations activities because they define who is important, influential or valuable as your startup works to drive brand awareness, a competitive presence and, of course, attract customers.

A target list can be created using a spreadsheet with the following fields:
- Name
- Publication
- Title
- Email address
- Telephone number
- Social media profiles (Twitter, Facebook, LinkedIn)
- Blog URL
- Website URL

- Interests
- Recent articles/posts

These lists can be built manually be adding new entries after reading relevant articles or blog post. You can also use these services:

- Google News and Google Alerts to discover reporters and bloggers writing about your company, competitors or industry. (Free)
- Buzzsumo, which lets you discover the most shared content across all social networks, as well as find influencers in any topic to see the content they are creating. (Free/paid)
- GroupHigh, which makes it easy to identify, manage and track bloggers. (paid)
- Vocus and Meltwater, which have databases featuring thousands of media members. (Paid)

Build relationships

Another pre-pitch activity is building relationships with reporters and bloggers. It involves activities such as following them and engaging with them on social media, commenting on their blog posts or articles, sending emails that offer industry insight and story ideas, asking them for coffee, or meeting them at conferences. The "return on investment" happens in a couple of ways:
1. When a reporter or blogger is looking for commentary or a quote, they usually turn to people that they know.
2. When it does come time to pitch your story, it's not a "cold call" because there is a relationship of some kind.

Creating a pitch

Okay, you have built a target list of reporters and bloggers. Give yourself a pat on the back. (Hey, it's good to celebrate small and big successes!)

Now what?

Next, you want to reach out to these people so they can, hopefully, provide coverage so your company basks in the spotlight to drive leads, sales, users, downloads, etc. This requires a media pitch. Much like a pitch to potential customers, a media pitch is designed to capture someone's attention so they want to learn more. It is a straightforward proposition but pitches need to be carefully crafted to not only be distinct and interesting but also stand above the dozens of other pitches received by reporters and bloggers every day. It is not enough to be new or interesting, you need to be unique, have a twist, or position yourself as relevant and newsworthy. And, as important, your pitches must be personalized to reflect the interests of a reporter or blogger. Nothing turns off a reporter or blogger more than a generic pitch that says "I didn't do any research so I have no clue about what might be news to you". I can count the number of times, for example, that I received a pitch that began with "Hi", "Reporter" or "Blogger" as opposed to "Mark".

Pitching reporters and bloggers requires a strategic and tactical plan. It makes no sense to blast out hundreds of pitches if many of them are immediately deleted, unread or deemed irrelevant. The creation of a pitch starts with putting yourself in the shoes of a reporter or blogger. What would make them say, "This could be an interesting story", other than your startup is new and/or doing something interesting? There is no lack of startups doing interesting stuff, so being interesting is not, well, particularly interesting. Instead, you need to focus on what makes your startup unique or different. Are you tackling a problem that hadn't been solved before? Is your product disrupting an established market or industry because it is faster, better, cheaper, etc.? Is there a compelling back-story about your startup's launch? Did your idea, for example, ignite when you got stuck in the elevator with a stranger, and emerged an hour later with an idea and partnership?

Depending on the people on the target list and their interests, a pitch can consist of a single theme or several variations. The core of the pitch stays the same but the introduction and key points can be tweaked to personalize them. A successful pitch, even if it does not lead to coverage, resonates because it talks to the interests of a reporter or blogger. Keep in mind, successful pitches can hinge on being in the right place at the right time (e.g. a slow news day), an idea that aligns with a story already in the works, or simply luck. Even if a pitch does not work, it can serve as a valuable stepping-stone for the next time you have a story to tell.

Here are a few tactical things to remember when pitching a reporter or blogger:

1. Use email as opposed to telephone calls, which can be disruptive.
2. Keep your pitch short - three or four paragraphs should do the trick.
3. Personalize the email. Use their first name. An email that starts with "Hi", "Blogger" or "Mr. Smith" is not only impersonal but it screams that someone did not do their homework.
4. Don't be too cute with the subject line. It is fine to be creative and intriguing but let your story do the talking.

Here's how you could structure an email pitch:

> *Subject: New Way to Track Customers*
>
> *Hey <First Name>,*
>
> *My name is [first name] from [company name]. Given your interest in new CRM services, I think you may be interested to hear more about our startup, which makes it easy for Gmail users to track sales opportunities and leads. Since our launch earlier this year, we have attracted XX,XXX users, including large companies such as X, Y and Z. Forrester analyst Bob Smith says we're the best CRM service since sliced bread.*
>
> *We are launching a new premium service next week. You can learn more about what we're doing at www.xyz.com/product. I would be happy to answer any questions.*
>
> *Thanks,*
> *Name, Title*
> *Contact Info: email, phone*

Bottom line - The pitch is:
- Personalized
- Aligned with the interests of the reporter or blogger
- Provides a snapshot of the product and, as important, context
- Offers options to learn more or contact the company

Creating a press kit

A press kit provides a snapshot of your startup but it does not need to be an extensive or super-detailed document. Given the demands on reporters and bloggers, few have the time to go through a large press kit. It means you are creating a briefing document that answers key questions, and sets the stage for further conversations. A press kit, which can be paper, digital or both, should consist of the following elements:

- A description of what your company does, who it serves, the benefits and what makes it unique
- Logos and screen shots
- Photos and bios of the founders
- A fact box about when the startup was created, number of employees, Website address, social media presence and contact information.

Here are two examples of online press kits that provide solid information in a user-friendly way:

The Gorge - http://thegorge.onlinepresskit247.com/media-coverage.html

STORYTELLING FOR STARTUPS

Balsamiq - http://balsamiq.com/company/press/#presskit

Tracking media outreach success

Like anything, you need to measure the performance of your efforts and campaigns. How many reporters and bloggers opened your emails, how many responded, how many links were opened, how much social media activity was generated, how many stories were written, etc.?

How can you tell if your emails have been opened and how often? Here is a list of free and paid tools that track email opens:
- Sidekick (getsidekick.com/)
- Yesware (www.yesware.com)
- Bananatag (bananatag.com)
- Mailtrack.io (mailtrack.io)
- Toutapp (toutapp.com)

Note: These services can tell if email is opened by automatically inserting a small transparent image into each message that the recipient can't see.

CASE STUDY: MEDIA OUTREACH

Media outreach involves a lot of grunt work. It is investing the time and effort to build relationships with reporters and bloggers who are inundated by startups looking for attention. So how can a startup rise above the crowd?

For Lior Degani, co-founder with Swayy, a content discovery startup in Tel Aviv, the recipe for getting coverage (more than 5,500 inbound links in the past year) has been persistence, doggedness and a willingness to continually connect with reporters and bloggers.

At the core of Degani's success is a database that is constantly updated. Every day, he tracks media coverage about the content marketing industry and Swayy's competitors to identify reporters and bloggers. This database contains the following information:

- Article URL
- Name of the writer
- Where it was published
- Post type: a review, list, leadership piece, etc.
- The post's focus
- The post's popularity
- The writer's email address, Twitter handle

Degani then sends emails to people on the target list. He uses a variety of subject lines to make sure they are relevant to the recipient. Degani introduces himself, explains why he is reaching out, and inserts a link to a deck, video or the product. Finally, he asks for their feedback and thoughts. "It's along the lines that 'I would love to hear your thoughts, and thoughts can be feedback about the product or thoughts on whether they find it useful, and whether they would find it useful for their readers. It is about being straightforward, which I recommend. You shouldn't be shy. If you are reaching out to people whose jobs is writing, it's okay to ask them if they would like to write about your company."

In addition to connecting via email, Degani takes a cross-platform approach in which he follows people on Twitter, retweets their content and engages in conversations. He will also leave comments on blogs, and reply to their newsletters. Then, Degani will continue to send them emails about new features and other news. While high-profile reporters and bloggers get a lot of attention from startups, Degani says it also pays off to reach out to smaller publications and blogs because this is where many "real" customers can be found.

KEY TAKEAWAY:

One of the keys to getting media coverage is doing the grunt work long before you need it. It is unglamorous work but it can eventually pay off.

"It is a no-brainer to do your own PR, especially in the early days because no one can tell your stories better than you. It's more authentic and more interesting. In general, people will care, which is the goal for PR for people to care about your story and get them interested and excited. If you can't get someone excited, that's a bad sign" - Robleh Jama, startup entrepreneur

KEY QUESTIONS:

1. What are your media goals?

2. Who do you want to target?

3. What kind of stories will attract their attention?

4. Will you do it yourself, or hire a freelance or PR agency?

5. How will you measure success?

> **EXERCISE**
> Create a spreadsheet, and add information about reporters and bloggers that could be part of a media outreach campaign. Put together a press kit that features a corporate description, screenshots and media contacts.

CHAPTER 14

The Secret Formula For Attracting Media Coverage

"If you don't like the news, go out and make some of your own."
- Wes "Scoop" Nisker

Want to know the secret to attracting media and blog coverage? I hate to break it to you, but it does not exist.

Getting coverage is not a science or an algorithm. There is no magical formula to attract the attention of reporters and bloggers like bees to honey. This is the honest truth from having spent 15+ years as a newspaper reporter. It is the insight that also comes from pitching the media and bloggers for startup clients. If a PR agency says it can guarantee media coverage, don't believe them. No one is that good, particularly when it involves coverage for an early-stage startup. Media and blog coverage happens for many reasons. Sometimes, it is a big announcement such as a large financing or an acquisition. Sometimes, it is an innovative, unique or different product that captures the imagination of a reporter. And sometimes, it is simply being in the right place at the right time, or getting lucky (sitting beside a reporter at a conference). In other words, there are multiple paths to getting media coverage and many ways for it to happen.

While media coverage is exciting and rewarding, it is important to remember it does not always lead to higher sales, particularly if your product has yet to be released or it is not fully baked. In many ways, media coverage is a bonus, not a silver bullet. Startups still need to focus on day-to-day marketing and sales programs to attract and convert customers.

So what are some of the key ingredients to get media coverage? Again, there is nothing that leads to guaranteed results but the most compelling themes include:

- Success
- Innovation
- Being new
- Have a twist
- Being different

- Raising money
- Relationships

Now that we have established the media coverage landscape, let's look at the different variables that could - and we are putting the emphasis on "could" - convince the media that your story is worth their attention.

1. Success: Everyone likes a good news story, particularly when it involves a small, scrappy startup that entices customers despite intense competition and a small marketing budget. The media loves success stories because they are sexy and exciting. And if a reporter or blogger happens to be the first person to put the spotlight on a successful startup, that can be a win-win proposition for the reporter and the startup.

CASE STUDY:

When Wave launched in 2009, Kirk Simpson, its CEO and co-founder, believed a free online accounting service was newsworthy given its major rivals - Xero, Intuit, etc. - asked people to pay. Armed with plenty of optimism and enthusiasm, Wave hired a PR agency to do media outreach. The result: no coverage. The problem: While Wave was a free service, it was entering a competitive market and it did not have enough users or credibility to be newsworthy.
Undeterred, Wave focused on improving the product and attracting new customers. Then, something incredibly lucky happened. On the same day that Wave hit the Google Chrome store, another product launched as well: Angry Birds. Riding the "rising tide lifts all ships" phenomenon, Wave started getting hundreds, then thousands of new users. Wave was suddenly newsworthy because it had serious traction…and credibility.

2. Raising money: If there is a slam-dunk for media and blog coverage, it is startups raising venture capital. To be honest, it really does not matter how much is raised - a small seed round or a monster "B" round. The media will likely cover it because money is a seductive creature and only a small number of startups are able to attract venture capital.

> **CASE STUDY:**
>
> Given the appetite for financing news, Hubba stood out from the crowd when it raised $1-million using a new crowdsourcing vehicle pioneered by Brightspark Ventures. It allowed 20 angel investors to participate in the deal through a new fund designed for the deal. The deal's structure made it more interesting to the media because it was a different type of financing.

3. Stories with a twist: One of the things that attract media and blog coverage are stories with an unusual slant or approach. These stories can be challenging to create because they are not black and white propositions such as raising money or attracting lots of customers. But they can be effective because they are different - and different can be a good thing.

> **CASE STUDY:**
>
> Brenton Hayden retired at 27-years-old. If that is not a story with a twist, then I don't know what is. The story emerged from work done by Onboardly, which was doing public relations for Renters Warehouse, the company that Hayden started. Hayden told Onboardly how he had been evicted from his apartment and

lost his well-paying job in the same week. He had spent two weeks sleeping in his car when the idea for Renters Warehouse emerged. Realizing this story had potential be an effective and unique, Onboardly pitched it to Entrepreneur.com. The angle was redefining "retirement", and how Hayden decided the wealth attained via Renters Warehouse would liberate him from work he hated, and let him do what he wanted. The story was published on Entrepreneur.com on January 27, 2014, and hit the homepage of Yahoo Finance the next day.

The results?
- On the day the story appeared, it was seen by 500,000 people
- In less than a week, there were more than 4,800 comments.
- It generated more than 576 solid leads in under two weeks.

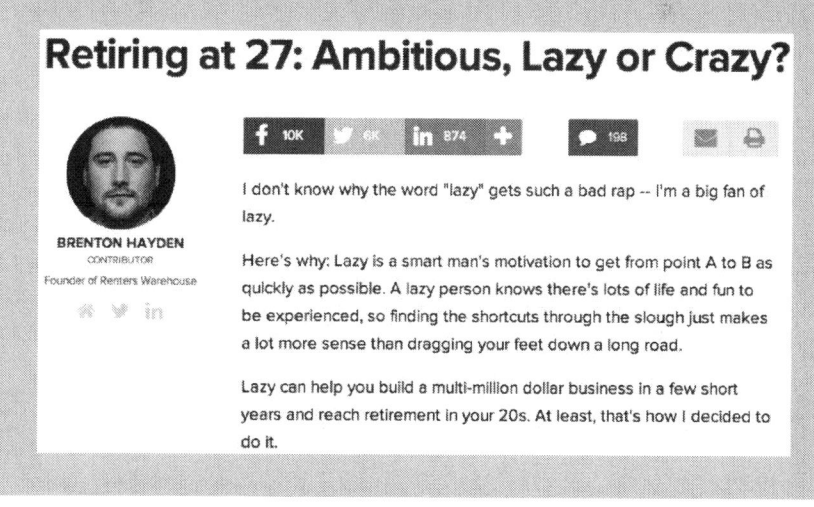

Retiring at 27: Ambitious, Lazy or Crazy?

BRENTON HAYDEN
CONTRIBUTOR
Founder of Renters Warehouse

I don't know why the word "lazy" gets such a bad rap -- I'm a big fan of lazy.

Here's why: Lazy is a smart man's motivation to get from point A to B as quickly as possible. A lazy person knows there's lots of life and fun to be experienced, so finding the shortcuts through the slough just makes a lot more sense than dragging your feet down a long road.

Lazy can help you build a multi-million dollar business in a few short years and reach retirement in your 20s. At least, that's how I decided to do it.

4. New and innovative: New is newsworthy. Everyone is curious about new products or services that seemingly come out of nowhere. The appeal of new and innovative is heightened when you can wrap it within an interesting narrative that makes it accessible and user-friendly. That is a powerful and newsworthy proposition.

CASE STUDY:

The brain is a fascinating and mysterious creature because no one knows how it functions. It explains some of the coverage around Muse, a band worn across the forehead that uses seven electroencephalography sensors to measure levels of brain activity. Developed by InteraXon, the technology is certainly innovative and fascinating, which explains the growing media coverage. It also helps that its co-founder Ariel Garten has become a well-known evangelist who can explain the technology in a user-friendly way.

5. Hijack the news: Sometimes, media opportunities come along when you are not expecting them. For all the planning to attract media coverage, a window can open when a major news event unfolds. It could be a big acquisition or an emerging trend involving other companies. The opportunities are inserting yourself into the conversation. It could be, for example, offering commentary or perspective about stories that reporters and bloggers see as valuable to enhance their coverage. This is one of the reasons why startup entrepreneurs need to position themselves as thought leaders and industry experts.

CASE STUDY:

As one of the leading online sticker makers, StickerYou was looking for ways to raise its profile. One of its new products was a sticker that could be applied to walls and sidewalks. With the 2014 World Cup happening, StickerYou CEO Andrew Witkin came up with an idea to get involved with a global story. He created sidewalk stickers for different countries, and placed them in different communities around Toronto supporting specific teams. StickerYou

> pitched a media story based on the idea it was giving people a new way to express their team loyalties. The result: A story in the Toronto Star, Canada's largest newspaper, that included StickerYou as one of four "offbeat" ways for fans to show their World Cup support (http://bit.ly/1pw8n6m)

6. Make yourself part of a bigger story: Too many startups try to make themselves the star of the story. Unfortunately, they are not that interesting, innovative or successful. Truth be told, it is really hard to get a reporter or blogger to write about a single startup, unless something makes it stand above the crowd. A better approach is being part of a bigger story. Let's say, for example, online accounting software for K-12 schools is gaining traction with school boards. A creative startup could seize the opportunity to develop a pitch about how school boards need better financial controls to deal with uncertain budgets and fraud. This is a more newsworthy story than a small startup with an interesting product.

> **CASE STUDY:**
>
> Within the financial services world, personal investment management is being disrupted. Once the purview of large firms that charged high fees, the market is being penetrated by innovative startups. Mike Katchen, founder and CEO with Wealthsimple, realized his startup could attract media attention by positioning itself as a Canadian pioneer for online investment management. He created a list of reporters and bloggers who wrote about financial issues, and served as advocates for consumers. To attract these reporters and bloggers, Katchen used a low-key approach. He tapped his network to see who could introduce him to the top five

or 10 people on his target list. Once an introduction was made, Katchen invited them for coffee to tell them about Wealthsimple. "The approach we took was approaching them as advocates for investors. We told them that 'we think you have a lot of helpful insight into what we want to accomplish. We want to build the best product, and the only way to do it is get feedback from people like you'. They were willing to spend a half hour with me to share their frustration about investment management and how we could fix it."
The result: Coverage in publications such as the Financial Post, MoneySense, ITBusiness, Sydney Morning Herald, Globe & Mail and Toronto Star.

7. Something different or weird: Sometimes, it pays off to pitch a story that goes against the grain, or it is just different or weird. These stories are fascinating because they stand out in the news stream from the same-old.

CASE STUDY:

Would you eat a cricket? It apparently has as much protein as beef, so why not. It is a story that got Norwood, Ont.-based Next Millennium Farms some solid media coverage as the only farm in North America that breeds, raises and processes insects for human consumption. You can't argue with the fact it is a different and strange story the media would find irresistible. Here is the story published in the Toronto Star - http://on.thestar.com/1y3vS8z

8. Build relationships with reporters and bloggers. Having personal relationships makes a huge difference. This can be done in the digital and analog worlds. It can start with following and engaging with a reporter or blogger on social media, sharing their content, and commenting on their blogs. It can involve sending email to reporters and bloggers with story ideas or insight. And, of course, relationships develop in the real world at coffee meetings, conferences, etc. One approach is sending an email asking a reporter or blogger for coffee. Tell them who you are, why you want to meet them, why they would be interested in what you are doing, and how you would be happy to meet near their office for a quick coffee. In other words, make it easy for them to say "yes". When I was a newspaper reporter, it took only one face-to-face meeting to create a relationship that created a win-win proposition for both parties.

A final thought about media coverage: It is exciting when it happens, and there is reason to celebrate and bask in the spotlight. But it is also a dividend, rather than the grand prize. In the scheme of things, however, news coverage is a happy bump along the way but it is unlikely to make your company a superstar. Startups that see a spike in traffic after getting covered by a high-profile Website such as TechCrunch, for example, are quickly shuttled to the sideline when the next "hot" story comes along.

KEY TAKEAWAY:

Attracting media coverage is part-art, part-science. To make it happen requires hustle, creativity, luck and timing.

"There are many different tools to tell the story. The first step is understanding your place in the world. " - Rebecca Reeve, founder and principal, Rsquared Communication

KEY QUESTIONS:
1. What makes your company or product newsworthy?
2. What is the story angle that you will pitch?
3. How will you approach reporters and bloggers?
4. What kind of stories do reporters and bloggers find interesting?
5. How do you track media outreach success?

EXERCISE

Brainstorm the different storytelling opportunities that your startup could pursue. Hold daily or weekly meetings to identify new opportunities.

CHAPTER 15

Picking the Time and Place for PR

"A good PR story is infinitely more effective than a front page ad"
- Richard Branson

To leverage PR or not to use PR, that is the question facing many startups looking to tell their stories to a wide audience. The value of PR is a mystery for startups because it is a process they do not understand. As important, PR costs money - something most startups are reluctant to part with. For most startups, however, PR is an intoxicating seductress. Startups lust after media and blog coverage because it is regarded as one of the most powerful ways to be validated. By capturing the spotlight - even if it is short-lived - startup entrepreneurs believe they can outflank the competition.

But there is a problem: attracting media coverage is not magical or a knockout punch. At best, it can provide a startup's marketing efforts with a huge shot in the arm. On the other side of the coin, there is also the danger of a startup thinking that media coverage means they have arrived. The reality is media coverage is a bonus, and something to be enjoyed and savored. But the spotlight will quickly shift to the next story, so startups need perspective about how much value media coverage actually delivers.

As someone who spent more than a decade as a technology journalist with national newspapers, I understand first-hand that startups need to be pragmatic and realistic about PR. This is particularly true for early-stage startups still trying to attract customers or refine their products. The biggest challenge facing most startups is they are not that newsworthy or innovative to successfully leverage PR. It is a harsh statement but there is so much competition for coverage that it is difficult to attract the spotlight without a great story. In too many cases, startups think an interesting product or a good idea is enough ammunition to justify PR. But without a compelling narrative, their PR efforts will falter.

DIY PR makes a lot of sense

For many startups, the most practical way to get started with PR is doing it themselves. To embrace the DIY approach to PR, there are many ways to improve the chances of success. Long before deciding to pitch a story to reporters or bloggers, you need to get ready. Over time, you should do the following:

1. Develop clear messaging about who you are, what you do, and who should hear your story (aka target audiences). Messaging is a key part of a startup's foundation because it powers their marketing and sales activities by making it easier for them to connect with target audiences (e.g. customers, partners, media and investors). Even if doing PR is not on a startup's radar, messaging will play a big role in their ability to get traction.

2. Create a target list that includes reporters, bloggers, influencers and analysts. It should include their names, email addresses, Websites, interests, information about the stories or posts they like to write, and their published stories and posts. (Note: There are more details about creating media lists in chapter 13.)

3. Build personal relationships. Although we live in an increasingly digital world, reporters and bloggers tend to write about people they know and like. It is human nature. It could start with a digital connection by leaving blog post comments, sharing insight and information via email, or following someone on social media. It could be analog by meeting reporters and bloggers at events, or asking them for coffee. When I was a reporter, it was interesting to see how quickly the dynamic of a relationship changed after a face-to-face meeting.

4. Create a press kit that provides a snapshot of what your company does, its history, customers, competitors, product screen shots, management bios, and contact information. The media kit can also include press releases, media coverage and social media links. (There is more information about how to create a press kit in chapter 13, as well as some examples.)

5. Get some media training. Many entrepreneurs have no experience with the media or bloggers, so they need to know the rules of engagement. Having insight into how reporters and bloggers operate sets the stage for a win-win proposition in which both sides get what they need. Media training also makes it easier for an entrepreneur to effectively tell their story and, as important, avoid mistakes.

CASE STUDY: DIY PR

With enough behind-the-scenes work, a startup's DIY PR efforts have a better chance of working. When it comes to pitching a story to the media, the best person is the founder or CEO because they have credibility and authenticity. When a founder/CEO reaches out, it is more personal and real. It is not a PR person looking for an editorial hit but a startup entrepreneur looking to tell their story. This resonates more with bloggers and reporters. Robleh Jama, founder of Tiny Hearts, a mobile app developer, says early-stage startups should do their own PR. "No one can tell your stories better than you," he says. "It's more interesting and more authentic. The goal of PR is getting people to care about your story and getting them interested. If you can't do it, that's a bad sign." Jama says one of the most important things about DIY

PR is getting ready long before you want to attract media and blogger coverage. Entrepreneurs, he says, who expect they can get coverage without preparing will be disappointed.

"To be successful, you need to start building relationships way earlier than you launch," he says. "You need to get involved with your industry, get involved in the conversation, and that means connecting with other companies in your industry, founders, bloggers, etc. You need to get involved, and you need to be relevant and know the relevant people whose voices are louder than anyone else. You need to be useful, be human, establish relationships, add value – don't just beg and ask; you need to give."

When Jama is looking to launch a mobile app, he said there are a few key steps:

1. He prepares for the launch three or four weeks in advance. This involves the creation of a list of reporters and bloggers to target.

2. It is important to craft a story about the new product. "A big part is why someone should care," he says. "What is the unique piece? Maybe we're doing 10 different things, but there could be one thing that people really care about. I'll focus on that piece because it resonates with people. You have to figure out the intersection of what makes your product unique, what people care about and what people are interested in."

3. It goes without saying, but it helps to have a great product or, at least, a product that delivers value. Jama points to Wake, an alarm app that Tiny Hearts created. The app attracted a lot of media coverage, which was a result of Jama's relationships with reporters and bloggers. But Jama said Wake is a great product with features that made it stand out from other alarm apps in the market. "The foundation of all good PR is a great product," he says.

When to leverage a PR agency

At some point, a startup has a good enough story and/or a big enough marketing budget to explore the use of external PR. The startup has arrived at a point where using PR will help take the business to the next level. They believe there is a good story to tell to a wider audience to drive brand awareness, search engine rankings, leads and sales.

Here are the biggest assets provided by a PR partner:

1. A Rolodex featuring relationships with key reporters, bloggers, analysts and influencers. In PR, these relationships are gold. They make it easier for PR people to get an audience for a startup's story. A PR person can use a personal relationship to break through the clutter and competition. This does not necessarily mean a startup's pitch will be embraced, but it may get some attention, which could lead to coverage.

2. The insight to pursue the right media outlets and blogs. In some cases, this can mean getting coverage that makes a business impact as opposed to widespread coverage that quickly fizzles.

3. The ability to develop and craft story pitches. Every story needs an angle or hook. It is hard to get media coverage by just having an interesting product. There are thousands of startups with interesting products, so a well-crafted pitch gives a story something different or unique to rise above the crowd.

When looking for a PR partner, the key questions to ask include:

1. What is their area of expertise?
2. What sectors do they know best?
3. Do they have experience with my product or sector?
4. Who are your clients? Can we talk to them?
5. Are you focused on B2B or B2C companies?
6. Do you have relationships with key reporters and bloggers? If so, who are they, and how well do you know them?
7. What are some of the publications that have covered your clients?

Rebecca Reeve, the founder and principal with Rsquared Communication, a PR agency in San Francisco, says one of the best ways to find the right PR partner is reaching out to entrepreneurs in the same space. "You need to make sure a third-party verifies and recommends a PR agency. The biggest indicator of success is prior success. Who have they worked with? What are the results achieved that align with what you are looking for? You need to view it as a long-term term thing. It is not something you can turn on and off. With a lot of the largest agencies, the VP sells a startup on a project, and then the VP only spends two hours a month on the account. You need to understand who is actually managing your account."

Establishing a PR partnership

Many PR agencies will want to create a long-term deal because the economics work in their favour. For startups, however, these deals may not be budget-friendly. In my experience, startups should probably date before they get married to a PR partner. An initial engagement could be two or three months, which is enough time for a media outreach campaign. Based on how well things go, a new agreement can be reached.

Another consideration is defining goals and success metrics. While it is impossible to guarantee coverage, it is judicious to establish expectations. It could be mentions in newspapers, magazines or blogs, as well as social media activity. At the end of the campaign, both sides can discuss and benchmark the performance by looking at the initial expectations. As important, startups need to be realistic about what PR can deliver. Even though a PR partner is getting paid, there is no guarantee coverage is going to happen. Truth be told, PR success often comes down to timing and luck. Even the best PR people need both, along with a good pitch and target list.

How to avoid PR mistakes

For startups diving into the world of PR, here is what not to do:

1. Fail to do enough research about the reporters and media to target. Startups need to know them inside out - their interests, favourite topics, stories they have written, places they have worked, etc.

2. Not understanding the power dynamic in which reporters and bloggers have the upper hand. In most cases, they decide what they want to write about. It means you need to play the game properly - sending well-crafted pitches, user-friendly collateral, review units (when applicable), etc.

3. Not dedicating enough resources after hiring a PR agency. It is not as simple as allocating a budget; startups need to support PR activity. This includes being available for brainstorming sessions, consulting decisions and interview opportunities.

4. Hiring a PR agency prematurely. As much as a startup wants to get going with PR, it has to understand being early is a mistake and a waste of time and money.

5. Having unrealistic expectations about what PR can achieve. In a blog post, *"Public relations is a Process not a Product Hunt"*, Chikodi Chima nails it when he says, "reporters are not algorithms to be optimized, or bugs to be squashed. Your favorite reporter is the smart, gorgeous girl everyone wants to be their prom date. She's not sitting around waiting for you to ask. She has a line of suitors from the front porch to the sidewalk."

Chima says setting expectations starts with well articulated PR goals and activities. "Some people do really well when they appear at conferences. Other people need to be in the consumer press or the mommy blogs. You need to focus on your customer acquisitions channels. When you're about to engage in a PR process, you need to be clear about how you define success and how you measure ROI. Getting a write up in TechCrunch is great, but if you need people to download your application hundreds of thousands of times, one article will not do it. You need a clear end game in mind."

Keep in mind that media coverage does not necessarily happen right away. It is often not as simple as reaching out to reporters and bloggers, and then watching the coverage roll in. In many cases, coverage can happen weeks or months down the road when your pitch or product becomes top of mind. It can happen because there is breaking news or a feature story. It can happen when there is a slow news day, which makes a reporter or blogger think about interesting pitches they might have received. The most important thing is having a good pitch that makes an impression.

> **CASE STUDY: CRAFTING A GOOD STORY**
>
> A key ingredient in doing public relations for a startup is timing - being in the right place at the right time with the right story.
>
> A good example of how to do it properly is ChannelMeter, which provides brands with in-depth analytics about how their videos perform on YouTube. The opportunity for ChannelMeter to insert itself into the spotlight emerged when South Korean singer Psy's *"Gangnam Style"* became a worldwide phenomenon with hundreds of millions of views on YouTube.
>
> Needless to say, there was a huge amount of media interest in the popularity of the video. With proprietary data about how the video performed, ChannelMeter was able to provide reporters and bloggers with unique news angles based on their specific interests. "We used *"Gangnam Style"* as a Trojan horse," said Chikodi Chima, who provided PR consulting services to ChannelMeter. "We were able to offer reporters and bloggers exclusives. We created stories using the same information we would give to everyone else, but customized to their unique needs."
>
> Chima said ChannelMeter's success in getting coverage not only hinged on having valuable data but packaging the story to different segments. Some media outlets such as Forbes and The Atlantic were interested in *"Gangnam Style"* as a news story, while other organizations such as ReadWrite wanted to focus on YouTube's power as a social media platform.

"We could have milked that forever," he said. "We were able to go to multiple outlets and give them a relevant story because we had thought leadership and domain expertise. We could come up with information that no one else had, and deliver unique insight that no one else could. We were able to come up with a lot of good angles for journalists."

KEY TAKEAWAY

There are different approaches to PR. In many cases, the DIY approach makes the most sense. The biggest value in using an agency is their ability to shape stories and access their relationships with reporters and bloggers.

"There are a million different ways to push a story so you can get a news push, achieve thought leadership, or get in front of VCs. Those goals influence the type of story you might be pushing at any particular time." - Rebecca Reeve, CEO, Rsquared Communication

KEY QUESTIONS

1. Why do you want to do PR? What are your goals?

2. When should you do PR internally versus hiring a PR agency?

3. Do you have relationships with bloggers and reporters?

4. Who would do the PR - internally, contractor, agency?

5. How are you going to measure your PR success?

> **EXERCISE**
> To prepare for a PR campaign, create a wish list of bloggers and reporters who could provide coverage. This list can be used for a DIY campaign, or be shared with a PR agency.

CHAPTER 16
How to Keep the Storytelling Machine Going

"Perseverance is not a long race; it is many short races one after the other"
- **Walter Elliot**

One of the most challenging aspects of story-driven marketing is keeping "the hits coming". It is one thing to dive into storytelling; it is another thing to keep it going on a regular basis. To be successful, story-driven marketing requires discipline, commitment and focus. It is accepting the reality that storytelling is a marathon, not a sprint. One of the keys to keeping the storytelling machine moving forward is having the structure and processes to create a high-performance "engine". It is easy for the excitement about storytelling to quickly disappear as people lose interest, and other projects and priorities emerge.

How can storytelling keep rumbling?

The storytelling machine is grounded in creating a culture that makes it clear that storytelling is a critical part of the corporate DNA. Storytelling needs to be seen in the same way as accounting, HR, marketing and sales – it is an integral part of the scenery and how business happens. Storytelling needs to be celebrated, encouraged and seen as one of the key tools for world domination….or something like that! At the same time, there needs to be a storytelling evangelist to keep everyone motivated, enthusiastic and striving for excellence. It could be the CEO, head of marketing or the social media manager. Whoever takes the lead, they are responsible for keeping everyone focused on the importance of storytelling to ensure the machine keeps going. This is an essential part of a structure that defines roles and responsibilities. Here is one way to look at the different players within the storytelling hierarchy:

1. The Storyteller in Chief: the person ultimately responsible for overall activity and success

2. The Storytelling Champion: the person who motivates, evangelizes and inspires

3. The Brainstormer: the person who helps to come up with new ideas and concepts

4. The Editor: the person who maintains quality control and editorial excellence

5. The Storytellers: the people who create stories on different mediums.

Within small companies, one person can have multiple "jobs", but it is important to articulate who does what. This ensures a collective ability to drive storytelling. At the same time, it holds everyone accountable for pulling their weight.

Okay, you have the enthusiasm for storytelling and the structure to drive it forward. What's next?

Before a company can launch itself into story-driven marketing, it needs to know what stories to create. Does it dive head-first into social media, pump out white papers and case studies, or create a series of videos? Without beating the drum too loudly about knowing your customers, storytelling is about knowing your customers: their needs, interests and how they want to consume information during the buying process. You need to have an ultra-clear understanding of their behaviour before making a purchase. This requires in-depth knowledge, which comes from talking to potential and existing customers, as well as doing research and a competitive analysis. In the process, you want to get a crystal-clear picture of what kind of stories will resonate with customers.

For a B2C company, the most effective storytelling could consist of being on Facebook and Twitter and creating videos.

Why? This is how your customers get information, so you need to party where the party is happening. As a result, it makes little sense to create white papers and case studies if they do not engage or motivate your customers. This may seem like a simplistic formula but, in some respects, storytelling is not rocket science. It is the old adage of giving people what they want.

And we talked about structure, didn't we? As much as storytelling is about creativity, agility and, heck, spontaneity, there needs to be a path to follow. This is not to suggest the path is always a straight line but it provides the way forward. One of the most valuable and effective "navigation" tools is the editorial calendar. It is a document - usually a spreadsheet - that, in simple terms, articulates who does what and when. An editorial calendar can be applied to any kind of marketing and sales content: blog posts, videos, white papers, case studies, e-books, etc. Just as having a storytelling evangelist is important, an editorial calendar is a great way to drive transparency and make everyone accountable because it spells out roles, responsibilities and actions. In many ways, it makes the storytelling process easier. This is particularly important for fast-moving companies where new priorities can suddenly become urgent priorities. Without an editorial calendar to provide structure and discipline, storytelling can easily fade into the background.

Here is an example of an editorial calendar (see below) created by HubSpot, an inbound marketing and sales company, that provides details about who is responsible for content, the deadline for its creation, the publishing date, the topic/title, the content, keywords, target personas and calls to action. It is a well-articulated plan that covers all the bases so nothing falls through the cracks.

While an editorial calendar is a valuable tool, it is just a tool that can be leveraged. When it comes down to it, storytelling happens on a regular basis when it becomes part of how the business operates. Storytelling is treated in the same way as sales; something that happens every day to move the ball forward. If storytelling does not have this stature, it will be a challenge to have any kind of success.

HubSpot	TOPIC/TITLE	CONTENT/DETAILS	KEYWORD(S)	TARGET PERSONA(S)	OFFER/CTA
MONDAY					
Author: Pamela Vaughan Due Date: 10/20/2012 Publish Date: 10/23/2012	12 Revealing Charts to Help You Benchmark Your Business Blogging Performance [NEW DATA]	Explain importance of blogging and how to benchmark your efforts to garuntee success	business blogging, blogging benchmarks	Owner Ollie, Mary Marketer	Free Report: Marketing Benchmarks from 7K Businesses
TUESDAY					
Author: Arum Hussa Due Date: 10/20/2012 Publish Date: 10/23/2012	Top SEO Tips Straight From the Industry Experts [INFOGRAPHIC]	Highlight SEO tips through expert advice while promoting complete guide	search engine optimization, SEO	Owner Ollie, Mary Marketer	Free Guide: Learning SEO from the Experts
WEDNESDAY					
Author: Maggie Georgieva Due Date: 10/20/2012 Publish Date: 10/23/2012	How to Craft the Right Questions for Your Next Marketing Survey	Use an excerpt from the Marketing Surveys ebook to provide readers beneficial survey best practices	marketing surveys, survey marketing	Owner Ollie, Mary Marketer	The Ultimate Guide to Using Surveys in Your Marketing
THURSDAY					

Source: http://offers.hubspot.com/blog-editorial-calendar

Remember to celebrate success

Another way to keep the storytelling machine rumbling is celebrating successes. We explored the challenges of attracting media coverage, so it is important to recognize and revel in it when it occurs. If there are people behind the scenes who played a key part in making it happen, they should be acknowledged. As important, the coverage should be shared internally and externally. Getting employees excited about media coverage is a great way to motivate them. At the same time, putting media stories in the spotlight via social media is an effective way to amplify the coverage. And it is not only media and blog coverage that should be celebrated. It is essential to put the spotlight on corporate blog posts that attracted a lot of traffic or comments, or white papers that were enthusiastically downloaded. Creating stories can be tough slogging and a lot of work, so it is a no-brainer to celebrate while, at the same, time recognizing the need to keep moving forward.

KEY TAKEAWAY:

Getting started with story-driven marketing is the easy part. The challenge is keeping things going. It is a marathon versus a sprint.

"There is no greater agony than bearing an untold story inside you." --Maya Angelou

KEY QUESTIONS:

1. Who are your internal and external storytellers?

2. How is storytelling structured and planned?

3. Who's the audience for your stories?

4. How do you create a storytelling calendar?

5. How do you track who does what when?

EXERCISE

Create an editorial calendar that includes all your marketing (and storytelling) activities. This spreadsheet should include the different options (e.g. blog posts, case studies, press releases), who is responsible for creating and editing them, when they should be published, and how they should be distributed.

CHAPTER 17

Tell, Don't Sell

"Content is fire. Social media is gasoline."
- Jay Baer, **marketing strategist**

Tell, don't sell.

It is a statement you hear all the time but what does it mean? How are telling and selling different? Storytelling is obviously about "telling", whereas selling often reflects what a salesperson wants to communicate to a potential customer to convince them to make a purchase. Telling and, for that matter, storytelling is not about closing deals. It has more to do with building relationships and trust, and engaging people in interesting and relevant dialogues. At some point, someone may decide to make a purchase but that process unfolds more naturally when an integral part of the process is a compelling narrative. Successful storytelling happens when a startup delivers customer-centric content that resonates with a customer's needs and interests. Marcus Sheridan, a well-known content marketing consultant, said stories can be easily and quickly created if a startup is obsessed with its customers' problems. "Storytellers tell people about things they didn't know, and describe it in a way that is understood by everyone. That is what a master storyteller does."

How do you tell, rather than sell?

The answer is creating content that draws people into your brand and products using the power of storytelling. The good news is there are many ways to tell a story, depending on a startup's product, market, competitors, target audiences and customers it wants to reach. It could be an engaging Website, an entertaining video, an informative case study, a thought provoking white paper, an engaging blog, talking at a conference… and the list goes on. This gives startups plenty of storytelling opportunities to drive marketing and sales.

As we discussed in chapter nine when looking at developing a storytelling strategy, the key is telling the right stories to the right people at the right time based on their needs, interests and goals. Without large marketing budgets, creating good stories is an effective way for startups to spread the word and attract attention. It allows startups to leverage creativity to outflank the competition and rise above the digital noise.

What does it take to create great content?

To be honest, it involves time, people (it helps to have someone who can develop content), consistency and ideas. In the scheme of things, the cost can be relatively modest but, over time, the ROI can be significant. What does content deliver? The benefits include:

 - Thought leadership: For startups looking to establish credibility and confidence, looking and acting smart and being engaged is invaluable. With little or no track record and few customers, startups that position themselves as creative, interesting and innovative thinkers have a better chance of being noticed and taken seriously.

 - Brand awareness: As we have talked about, good stories are intriguing, sexy, compelling and interesting. If a story can capture someone's attention, it provides a startup with a great way to capture the spotlight, even it is only for a short period of time. You want people to talk about your stories because, in the process, they will talk about your brand and products.

 - Search engine optimization: For many startups, SEO can be a mystery and a challenge. Yes, your Website should be optimized (using WordPress can make SEO a lot easier), but you want to be ranked high for certain keywords when people are searching for information. One of the key benefits of storytelling in different ways is it generates keyword-rich and appealing content that can move your startup up the search rankings.

 - Leads and sales: Every company needs to drive leads down the sales funnel. No leads = no sales = no business. When a startup creates good content, one of the biggest benefits is it increases the chances of getting into a buyer's consideration funnel. This is the place where they begin to collect information about different products to meet their needs. In many respects, storytelling is about educating customers about the value of your products. Marcus Sheridan said his pool installation company survived the 2008/2009 economic downturn by creating videos and blog posts that answered questions about buying and maintaining a pool. (Note: As Sheridan created videos and blog posts, he established himself as one of the top content marketing experts. It was a classic case of leading by example!)

- Drives social media activity: Jay Baer, a marketing strategist, says "content is the fuel, social media is the road". For startups looking to leverage social media to attract attention and engage with target audiences, there is no better ammunition than high-quality content. A startup's social media efforts are more effective when there is content that delivers a combination of information, insight, opinion and guidance.

What kind of stories should be created?

With a wide variety of storytelling options, how do startups decide on the content to be created? It starts with a focus on creating high quality content. There is so much competition and so much content being produced that simply going through the motions is a recipe for failure. As a rule, I would suggest that less is often more. It is better to do a few things really well, rather than do many things in a mediocre way. This sounds like straightforward advice but far too often startups get suckered into doing too much to attract attention. In the end, their content delivers little value so it fails to make a positive impression.

The next step is developing content that plays to the needs, habits and interests of customers. It means content that is relevant, topical and accessible. As a rule of thumb, content should do one or more of the following: engage, educate and entertain. It is also necessary to create content that target audiences want to consume. It makes no sense, for example, to create terrific white papers or have a vibrant Facebook page if target audiences have little interest in white papers or Facebook. Still, many startups are guilty of missing the mark because they follow a misguided "create it and they will consume" approach to content.

This scenario always reminds me an episode on "WKRP in Cincinnati" (a popular television sit-com in the 1970s) in which Jennifer Marlowe, the radio station's receptionist, decides to provide Herb Tarlek, the sales manager, with a wardrobe refresh. While Herb's new clothes look great, his customers don't trust him because he no longer looks like them. This prompts Herb to go back to his plaid suits, white belt and white shoes. The key takeaway from Herb's clothing adventure is the importance of connecting with target audiences, even if means doing things that are not sexy, hip or shiny. It does not mean a startup should not take risks by being creative, but it has to take into account what the audience finds interesting and relevant.

Who should create stories?

For startups, one of the biggest storytelling challenges is deciding who creates stories and content. Usually, there is not anyone in-house with the skills or expertise given product development and sales are bigger priorities. But as startups embrace storytelling, a key part of strategic planning is figuring out who drives the engine. Here are a few options:

1. The bare-bones approach is recruiting someone internally to become the "marketing" person or storyteller. This is someone who has writing skills, although it might not be their job or calling. A key asset is good communication skills so they can easily tell a story or supervise the creation of stories. To be honest, this is a short-term proposition because it is like trying

to squeeze a round peg into a square hole. It will work for a while but, at some point, it will become obvious that more expertise is needed.

2. Hiring someone part-time or on contract is like dating without getting married. It can be a win-win approach because the marketer gets the opportunity to work on a cool project, while a startup does not have to make a long-term commitment or provide benefits, stock options, etc. Another benefit of using contractors is it provides a startup with the opportunity to have good stories created and learn more about its marketing/storytelling needs. As a marketing strategy is developed, the required skills start to emerge. These skills could align with the person being used, or they could suggest using someone with different expertise.

3. Use online content services such as Digital Sherpa, Contently or BlogMutt that offer strategic, tactical and distribution services. These services make it easy to generate content for blogs, white papers and case studies but you need to supervise and offer guidance about tone and topics to be covered.

4. Hiring a full-time marketer is the biggest leap, or seems that way. It means bringing on someone with unique skills, needs and objectives. It can be challenging because marketers are different creatures - they talk and operate differently. To hire the right person, one of the keys is being sure of the skills and experience needed, and the type of person who would fit into your corporate culture. Given the importance of hiring a marketer, it makes sense to be patient rather than jumping into the fray. Some of the questions to ask include:

1. Do you have experience with the marketing channels we want to use?
2. What are your writing, communication and social media skills?

3. Do you have any experience with blogging, Website design, analytics or marketing tools?
4. Have you worked with a startup, or operated in a fast-moving environment?
5. Do you have any experience with our industry/market?
6. Do you have the ability to provide strategic counsel and tactical execution? It is important to stay away from marketers who want to tell but not do.
7. Do you have an appetite to do other things such as social media, business development, sales presentations and media outreach?
8. What are the skills that make you the right fit to work at a startup?

The need to prioritize

Faced with a buffet of content options, it is important to prioritize to achieve your goals and objectives. In an ideal world, a startup would do everything, but that would require having the people, money and time - something startups tend not to have. As a result, startups need to put together a plan to create content in phases. For example, a startup looking to drive sales might decide the content that moves customers into the sales funnel is a Website with strong calls to action, sales decks and one-pagers. It means not doing a blog, infographics or white papers, but sometimes you can't be all things to all people at the same time. In time, a startup can expand its storytelling "portfolio" as sales grow and it can add more resources. It comes down to being strategic and deciding what is going to deliver the best bang for the buck.

In the next chapters, we will explore the different storytelling options. There are plenty of books and online sources that get into the tactical nitty-gritty, so we will take a high level approach and focus on best practices, good tools and real-world case studies of storytelling in action. This will provide you with a good grasp of the key concepts, fundamentals and the road to success.

KEY TAKEAWAY:

Focus on content that involves a story and meets the interest of customers. It's the best way to engage, educate or entertain.

"Content is King" - Bill Gates

KEY QUESTIONS:

1. Why create content?

2. What kind of content will you create?

3. Who will create content?

4. How will it be published?

5. How will it be shared and publicized?

EXERCISE

Have a corporate-wide brainstorming session to create ideas for content and storytelling. This should include founders, marketing and sales people, account managers, customer support reps, and support staff. Ask everyone to provide the questions asked by existing and potential customers.

CHAPTER 18
An Insider's Take on Storytelling

"For someone with more than 30 years in the business, there has never been a better moment for folks like us. The audience has spoken. They want stories. They're dying for stories."
- Kevin Spacey

Storytelling is exciting because there are many ways it can happen. And it does not matter about a startup's size, or whether the market is B2B or B2C. At the end of the day, it comes down to having a passion and commitment to storytelling, and investing the time, people and creativity to make it happen. It explains why many startups can knock off large incumbents by telling better stories.

As we mentioned earlier, storytelling is not a one-size-fits-all proposition. What works for one startup may not work for another due to the customer mix, a product's benefits and features, the competitive landscape, or the market's maturity. With research into target audiences and the ability to craft customer-centric stories, you can get a strong handle about the stories to tell and where to tell them. It is important to remember, however, there is no such thing as a perfect plan of attack. Like anything, there are many variables that impact success, which means stories may have to be tweaked, edited or overhauled to make them work better.

So, let's start to look at the different ways to tell stories.

You can call them channels, vehicles or marketing opportunities. The common denominator is they are ways to engage, educate and entertain (aka the three E's) with target audiences. We are going to focus on defining each opportunity, provide case studies that offer real-world insight, highlight best practices and make recommendations about the tools to use. Each section will provide a better sense of what is involved to create stories so you can embrace a do-it-yourself approach, or have the insight to hire the right people.

CHAPTER 19:
The Building Blocks for Websites That Work

"A great website design is so much more than just delivering content and making it look good. When visitors come to your site, they produce a set of feelings about your website and your organization."
- **Amber Leigh Turner**

In simple terms, Websites are a startup's digital doorway. All the time, money and effort spent to drive people to your Website hinges on giving people the information, encouragement and guidance to get them to do something. It could be registering for a service, contacting you, downloading software, signing up for a Webinar or a newsletter, learning more about how your products work, attending an event, or making a purchase. Whatever the goal, you need to make it abundantly clear what a potential or existing customer should do.

Think of it this way: When someone visits your Website, it is a great marketing and sales opportunity. They have made an investment to visit; now it is your turn to capitalize by getting them to do something that is a win-win for both parties. And here is a key point: people are lazy on the Web. They do not want to do any work, so unless you blatantly tell them to do something, they won't do anything, other than click away, which completely negates your marketing efforts.

As a result, Websites need to be well-oiled digital engines that efficiently and seamlessly let people get information, make purchases, etc. To make that happen, people should interact with your Website without doing much thinking. It should just work. And, as important, Websites need to grab someone's attention quickly. According to eye-tracking research done by the Missouri University of Science and Technology, it takes users less than two-tenths of a second (yes, that is less than one second!) to form a first impression. That is a huge challenge, but it highlights the importance of a well-designed Website with clear messaging and strong calls to action and, of course, good stories.

"Your Website is your biggest tool, it's your store and public face so you have to make sure what you say, how you say it and how it looks really resonates with target audiences," says Stuart MacDonald, a business advisor. "Before spending money on advertising or social media, the first thing to do is make sure your Website is easy to use, and that when someone shows up, they understand you get them and their problems."

While there is plenty of buzz about the benefits of marketing that drives people to your Website (aka inbound marketing), many companies simply stop marketing to consumers after they attract them to their Websites. It is strange given the effort involved to draw visitors, but too many companies believe the marketing battle is over when, in reality, it has just begun.

Here are some best practices to ensure your Website is a marketing and sales machine rather than the place where inbound traffic goes to die.

Messaging: In a multi-tasking, attention-deficit world, clear messaging is crucial. On the Web, first impressions happen quickly so your messaging must resonate; otherwise a golden opportunity is lost. Messaging has to deliver the following: what your product does, who should use it, and the key benefits. That is a lot of information in few words. Take a look at how Pipedrive, a CRM tool for managing sales, presents this information. The headline tells you what the product does. The sub-headline talks about the value delivered, while the benefits appear in the bottom right-hand corner.

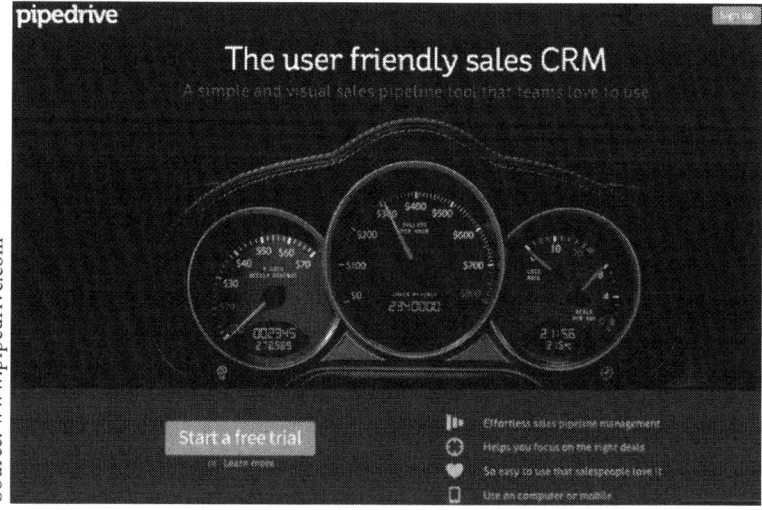

Source: www.pipedrive.com

Another good example is Pocket, which makes it easy for people to see what it does (bookmark content to read later), how to learn more, and how to sign up.

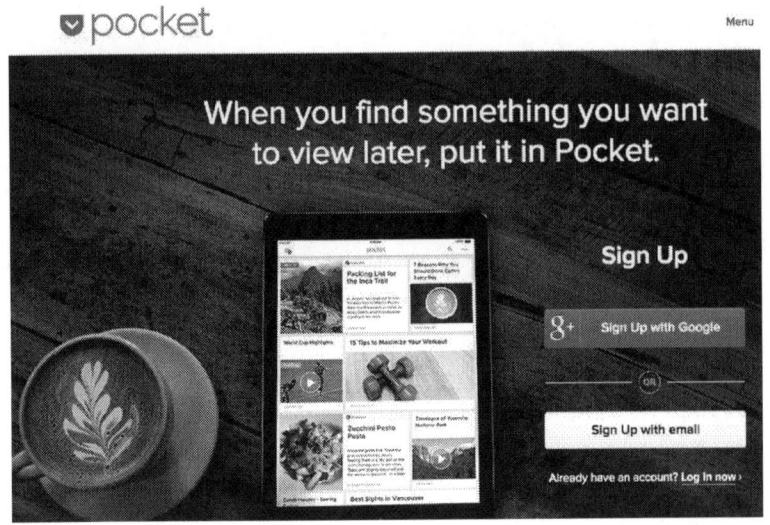

Source: www.getpocket.com

Navigation: Even if there is clear messaging and engaging content, it goes for naught if it is difficult to navigate a Website. It is like giving someone a car but not providing them with a steering wheel, let alone a GPS. Many Websites stumble by offering too many navigation options or unclear options. This causes confusion, which increases the likelihood of people leaving. Instead, Websites need navigation that flows and seamlessly moves people without it appearing like work. Each navigation option has to be intuitive so it is easy to discover information. Another key is gradually offering more options as people flow through the Website, rather than having everything available at the beginning of the journey. Here is an example of user-friendly navigation from Punk Ave. Each option lights up when hovered over, and offers some details of what to expect.

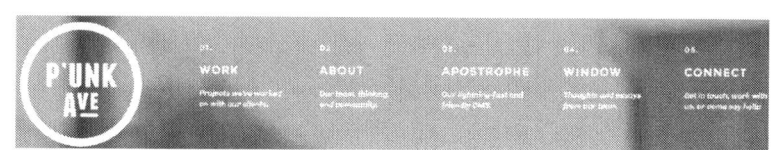

Source: www.punkave.com

Design: Ugly Websites are a recipe for disaster. But there are plenty of examples of terrible Website design being allowed to escape into the wild. As much as good content and navigation is important, design is as crucial because it sets the mood and tone for Website visitors.

When people are browsing or seeking instant gratification, good design is vital. If a Website's design is compelling, it is a snap for people to get engaged and excited. As important, design has to drive a Website's goals. On an e-commerce Website, for example, design must encourage the sales process or, at least, get someone more interested in making a purchase. Look at how RØDE uses clever design to help customers purchase a microphone. Rather than make someone click on a specific microphone to see if it meets their needs, RØDE asks them to complete two fields - what they want to use the microphone to do (record, amplify) and how they want to use it (sing, podcast, interview, presentation, etc.). By using smart design, RØDE eliminates a lot of work and makes it easier to make a purchase.

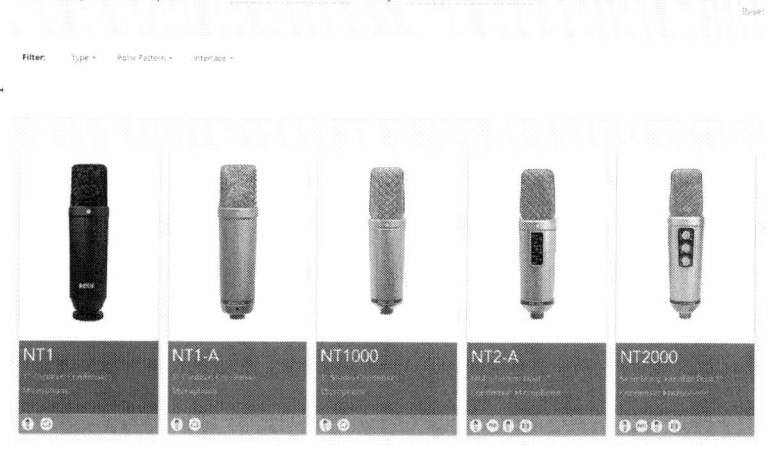

Source: www.rodemic.com/microphones

Calls-to-action: So people arrive at your Website and check out a bunch of content, but they don't do anything "significant". They do not make a purchase, download a white paper, read a blog post or ask for a demo. Why? It is probably because there was nothing on the Website that specifically told people what to do. It sounds like a straightforward proposition but, as we noted earlier, people are lazy. It means you have to overtly tell people what you want them to do. If you want them to download a white paper, have a call-to-action that says, "Download a free white paper". If you want them to see a product demo, have a call-to-action that says, "Want to Learn More? Ask for a demo". It is pretty obvious, right? But telling people to do something is a good way to get them to do the things you want! Here is how CrazyEgg uses a call-to-action to encourage people to check out its service by tempting them with a free trial and a promise to boost their Website's conversion rates and revenue.

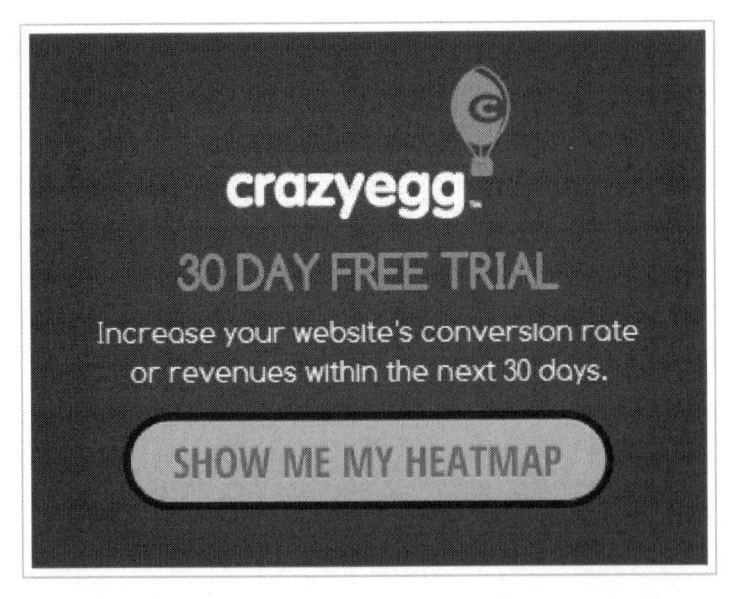

crazyegg

30 DAY FREE TRIAL

Increase your website's conversion rate or revenues within the next 30 days.

SHOW ME MY HEATMAP

Source: www.crazyegg.com

Easy to understand About pages

Often seen as an after-thought on many Websites is a company's "About" page. In many cases, this content is slapped together or a mishmash of different ideas. That is a mistake because an "About" page is one of the most effective and important storytelling vehicles on a Website. It is where a startup quickly tells people what it does, the problems it solves and the customers served, as well as information about the founders and corporate history. It is an ideal opportunity for a startup to establish credibility, spark interest, and demonstrate creativity. A good "About" page does not have to be long but it should be clear, engaging and accessible.

Here are some good examples of good "About" pages:

Moz uses design and creativity to tell its story in a visually compelling way. By scrolling down the page, you can see a timeline of the company's history to provide context about how it has grown over the years. This enhances Moz's credibility and provides customers with more confidence.

Source: www.moz.com

Twitter's About page is accessible, colourful and informative. The live stream on the right-hand side gives people a taste of the product, while three target audiences are given a quick overview of the specific benefits.

About Twitter

Twitter helps you create and share ideas and information instantly, without barriers.

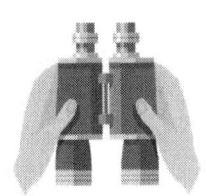

Getting started

Twitter is the best way to connect with people, express yourself and discover what's happening. Get started here.

Take Twitter with you

Go to about.twitter.com/products to get Twitter on your mobile device.

Twitter for business

Businesses use Twitter to share information about their services, gather real-time market intelligence, and build relationships with customers, partners and influencers.

Tweets

Twitter Sports
@TwitterSports
From tailgates to touchdowns, the pulse of #SB49 was alive on Twitter:
blog.twitter.com/2015/the-new-e...
pic.twitter.com/TQFBzGz1pv
Retweeted by Twitter
Show Photo

Source: about.twitter.com

PEEP LAJA'S FIVE WEBSITE PRINCIPLES

When it comes to having an effective Website, Peep Laja (conversionxl.com/) believes there are five key principles: relevancy, clarity, value, friction and distraction. Here is how he defines each principle:

- Relevancy: Does the page meet the user's expectations – both in terms of content and design? How can it match what they want even more?
- Clarity: Is the content/offer on a Website page as clear as possible? How can we make it clearer and simpler?
- Value: Is a Website page communicating value to the user? Can we do it better? Can we increase user motivation?
- Friction: What on this page is causing doubts, hesitations and uncertainties? What makes the process difficult? How can we simplify?
- Distraction: What on the page is not helping the user take action? Is anything unnecessarily drawing their attention? If it is not a motivation, it is friction.

Laja, a conversion optimization expert (aka he makes Websites work better), says embracing these principles ensures a Website performs and helps a company achieve its strategic and tactical goals. It starts with ensuring that every page has a singular focus – whether it is making a purchase, signing up for a service, downloading software or asking for a demo. To motivate people to take an action, Laja says it is important to minimize distractions. This means stripping down a page so people are not tempted to do other things such as watch a video or read content.

Motivation is also an important consideration. If you want someone to do something, Laja says they need encouragement and good reasons to be engaged. "Are we doing enough and can we do more to increase motivation? Are we talking about benefits?

> Are we telling them what their life will be like after they use our service?" To keep people motivated, Laja says friction has to be eliminated. Friction prevents people from completing an action because the process is not seamless. It could be unclear and inaccessible design, or confusing navigation.
>
> "To get people to take action, you need to increase motivation and decrease friction – this makes it easier to take action. Sometimes, we put up with crappy Websites with lots of friction because motivation is so high. Yesterday, for example, I was buying a strange tea, and I was extremely motivated. The Website was terrible but my motivation was so high, I forgave all the bad stuff. Sometimes, you are not motivated but it is so easy to do something. When it comes to reducing friction on a page, you need to understand the objections people have."

Tool Kit:

There are thousands of tools to create and optimize Websites. Here are a few of the most popular:

- **WordPress:** The world's most popular content management system, powering more than 75 million Websites in 120 languages. WordPress is open source software that can be downloaded at no cost at www.wordpress.org. There is also a large developer community, which has created more than 30,000 plug-ins that make it easy to add new features and functionality to a Website - many of them free or at a nominal price.
- **Squarespace**: A software-as-a-service platform to quickly launch Websites and blogs with little technical or design knowledge. It is also affordable with prices ranging from $8 to $24/month.
- **Crazy Egg**: A service that shows how people are

behaving on your Website - where they are clicking, what they are reading or watching - through heat maps and scroll map reports.
- **Optimizely**: A user-friendly service to do A/B testing to perform experiments on your Websites to improve its effectiveness and performance.
- **KISSmetrics** gives you deep customer knowledge by identifying who's in each step of your funnel so that you can reach out to them in a more meaningful way

CHAPTER 20

Celebrating Your Customers' Success

"An organization's ability to learn, and translate that learning into action rapidly, is the ultimate competitive advantage."
- Jack Welch

Definition of a case study: "A documented study of a specific real-life situation or imagined scenario, used as a training tool in business schools and firms."

By and large, case studies are not terribly sexy but it does not mean they have no value. Case studies are solid marketing vehicles because they are stories that celebrate the customer and how their problems are addressed. In other words, they put the customer's success in the spotlight. Startups should embrace case studies to establish credibility and make potential customers more confident. As important, case studies are a key part of the sales process. In Eccolo Media's 2014 B2B Technology Content Survey Report, case studies were ranked third by customers when evaluating a technology purchase. White papers and product sheets topped the list.

The format for a case study consists of three elements:

1. The challenge/problem: What the client looking to achieve to drive their business forward.

2. The solution: How your product met their needs or challenges, and the process to position the product for success.

3. The results and conclusion: This is led by the benefits (e.g. sales, leads, efficiencies, etc.) generated. If a client is willing to give you metrics or numbers, that is a great way to quantify success. If numbers are not available, you can provide anecdotal evidence.

To create case studies, here is a recipe for success:

1. Identify the most interesting themes or stories, rather than writing about a particular customer. It could be how your product saved a customer a lot of money, helped them attract more Website visitors, or sparked a flurry of leads. These are stories that resonate with potential customers because they talk to their specific needs or interests.

2. Categorize the types of customers that have been successful with your product. This makes it easier to deliver a variety of stories that could connect with potential customers based on how your product meets their needs. Focus on getting your best or most interesting customers involved – customers who love your product and get value from it in different ways.

3. Create a list of questions to ask customers. These could include:

- How did you learn about our product?
- What products were you using before?
- How do you use our product?
- What are the biggest benefits?
- What features do you find particularly valuable?
- Can you provide an example of how it works for you?
- Have you discovered new or different uses for the product?
- Does the product deliver good value?

4. Case studies are effective when they are short and sweet – 350 to 800 words. This makes them accessible and user-friendly. No matter how good a case study, few people will

read a document that requires them to make a big investment.

5. Design is important to inject sizzle – things like eye-catching colours, information boxes, pull quotes and other elements to encourage people to read case studies. Many companies fail to do case studies justice by not giving them any design love – and we have all seen boring black and white examples. Look at using the term "Success Stories" to make case studies more appealing.

6. Promote and distribute case studies. Put them on your Website, create digital and paper-based versions to share with potential customers, share them with customers that are profiled, and include them in blog posts and newsletters.

Ben Plomion, ex-vice-president of marketing with Chango, said case studies are valuable because potential customers, particularly in the B2B market, usually go through extensive research, qualification and selection phases. "It's important for a vendor to quickly establish credibility through third party validation (show don't tell). Third party validation can be provided by industry organizations, trade publications or clients' case studies/success stories. Case studies are great because they establish expertise reported by buyers, and they can speed up sales cycles. The secondary benefit of case studies is they can help reporters and, to some extent, employees. Truly understand the value a company brings to clients."

Plomion said Chango is fortunate its clients are marketers who are tired of traditional one-page case studies. "We spend a lot of time designing great looking case studies that make our clients heroes, and that prospects enjoy reading. Great looking case studies that put our clients in the centre of the action are easier to get approved. It also helps to have killer design. We put case studies into a picture frame and send them to clients. Some clients put these case studies on their walls, or even send them to their mothers. And who wants to disappoint a marketer's mom?"

Here is a case study that shows how Lego used Chango's advertising technology to drive conversions and engagement via Facebook news feed ads. A compelling element is Chango's use of eye-catching design to put the spotlight on the results.

LEGO®'S $5 CPA ON FACEBOOK EXCHANGE

LEGO® Brand Retail partnered with Chango to become one of the first major brands to market through Facebook Exchange (FBX) News Feed ads. The results? They achieved a $5 Cost Per Acquisition (CPA) and exceeded all goals on order size.

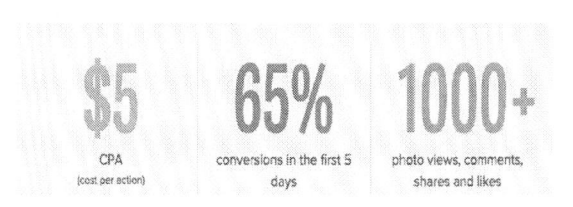

$5 CPA (cost per action)

65% conversions in the first 5 days

1000+ photo views, comments, shares and likes

Source: www.chango.com/results

Another startup leveraging case studies is GroupHigh, which offers an online service to discover, manage and track bloggers. GroupHigh uses the "classic" approach: introduction, the challenge and the solution.

GroupHigh Case Studies

Lorna Jane Finds More Influencers With GroupHigh

With a goal of creating meaningful and long term relationships with influencers to increase brand awareness, Lorna Jane needed to grow their digital outreach program. They found their answer in GroupHigh's online blog intelligence software. In just four months, Lorna Jane has seen amazing results.

GroupHigh has fueled an increase in the amount of bloggers Lorna Jane has formed relationships with and has aided in a boost in response rates all while reducing the time and effort required to identify bloggers.

Lorna Jane is runway-inspired active wear designed by women, for women. A recent arrival to the United States, Lorna Jane has more than 150 retail locations throughout Australia, South Africa, and America. The company's mission is to inspire women worldwide to live their best active life.

The Challenge

Lorna Jane is working to expand its brand internationally by reaching out to mid-level influencers in the form of bloggers.

Before having access to GroupHigh, Lorna Jane found influencers "in a very adhoc and uneven way. We would stumble across a possible influencer on Twitter or YouTube. This worked okay but it was neither consistent nor scalable." They knew there were many bloggers that were the perfect fit but Lorna Jane's team just didn't have the time or resources to find them.

Lorna Jane also found that keeping track of the bloggers they found, contacted and formed relationships with was an unorganized task. "We created lots of spreadsheets and spent days compiling blogger lists across Google. It was inefficient, time consuming and hard to keep updated."

The Solution

To help with all of their influencer outreach pain points, Lorna Jane didn't need more manpower or spreadsheets; they needed a tool to:

Using the right approach, case studies can be an effective part of a startup's sales and marketing efforts. They are powerful ways to show the world how your product provides value to customers. This makes case studies convincing at a time when there are many competitive options. While customers make purchase decisions based on benefits, features or price, they also need assurance and validation that a product delivers.

CASE STUDY: CROWDSOURCING CASE STUDIES

shopify What if a company decided to crowdsource its case studies rather than create them internally? It is an unorthodox approach but this is the path taken by Shopify to showcase the success of customers using its popular e-commerce platform to create online stores. To see if there was interest in the crowdsourced concept, Shopify invited 120,000 storeowners to submit a case study that, if selected, would be published on the corporate blog, along with a link to their store. More than 1,500 customers replied with stories about why they launched their stores, the things that made them successful, and recommendations for people thinking about jumping on the e-commerce bandwagon.

Mark Hayes, head of communications with Shopify, says a freelancer reviews the submissions, and then turns the best ones into blog posts, which feature images and links. "We are publishing 60 user-generated case studies every single week," he says. "You can't create that amount of high-quality content in-house. It is coming from the mouths of storeowners who are talking about their own businesses. They get a link and we tweet the case studies. It is a win-win situation."

Here is a case study published on Shopify's Website by Greats, an online shoe retailer.

How New Ecommerce Shoe Company Greats Brand is Aiming to Become the Warby Parker of Footwear

What do you get when you combine premium-quality, stylish sneakers at prices much lower than the competition? The answer is GREATS Brand - a new direct to consumer ecommerce shoe company that's aiming to disrupt the shoe industry by become the Warby Parker of footwear.

CHAPTER 21

Using Videos to Pack a Punch

"I'm sure if Shakespeare were alive today, he'd be doing classic guitar solos on YouTube."
- Peter Capaldi

There are many ways to tell stories, but among the most engaging are videos. They are a captivating way to tell the world what you do and why they should be interested – usually in 120 seconds or less.

Why video?

The most obvious reason is people like videos, which is not surprising given we live in a 500-channel TV world (although Bruce Springsteen suggests "there's nothing on"), as well as endless video options on the Web through services such as Netflix, YouTube and Vimeo. Given the choice between reading text (even beautifully crafted copy) and watching a video, I suspect 80% to 90% of people would pick a video. Videos are user-friendly because people believe there is less work involved, which is a big consideration for people who are time-strapped and multi-tasking. If done well, a video can deliver a wealth of information, while seemingly not requiring people to invest much time or brainpower. Videos also have "curb appeal", which is important given most people make quick decisions when they visit a Web site. "Video has a great way of packing of a lot of information into less time," says Lee LeFever, co-founder Common Craft, which has produced explainer videos for fast-growing startups such as Twitter and Dropbox. "There is a combination of a voiceover, something presented to you in a natural voice, combined with visuals that are moving that creates a situation where it is greater than the sum of the parts."

Videos also deliver excellent ROI because they can be used in many ways. For budget-conscious startups, which see any marketing expenditures as painful, getting bang for the buck with video is an attractive proposition. Here are some of the places where videos can be used:

- Websites (Home, About, Resources, FAQ)
- Presentations (sales, marketing, investment)
- Landing pages
- Newsletters
- Social media
- Investor pitches

There are three kinds of videos that can be used to tell stories:

1. Animated: In the past few years, animated videos have become all the rage. In fact, you could argue they have become too popular given nearly every startup seems to have one. Animated videos are widespread because they are accessible and entertaining, and perhaps tap into our childhood days of cartoon watching! A video can also deliver a lot of information about a product, the benefits and features. And animated videos don't have to cost a lot of money. They can be sourced inexpensively (<$1,000) using online services such as VideoHive.net or Promoshin.com, created internally by someone with good computer graphic skills, or outsourced for $1,000 to $5,000.

2. Live-action: The upside of a video featuring people is it creates a real connection with the audience. If a video involves a startup's founders and employees, it can deliver insight into corporate culture and its brand personality. In a world in which first impressions are so important, a well-made video can create brand affinity. As for cost, there is a wide spectrum. It can be cost-effective with the right equipment and some editing skills. It can also be expensive if you use professional videographers and talent.

3. Screencasts: To show target audiences your product first-hand in a cost-effective way, screencasts are a great option. They may not be the sexiest way to tell a story but they give people tangible information about how your product looks, feels and works. Screencasts are an effective way to talk about a product's benefits and features, which is why they are particularly popular for tutorials. As important, screencasts can be created easily and inexpensively using software such as Camtasia, Jing or Screencast-O-Matic.

Best practices for creating videos:

1. Keep them short: Most videos should be 45 to 180 seconds. A study by Wistia, a video hosting service, found that the longer a video lasts, the less it is viewed.

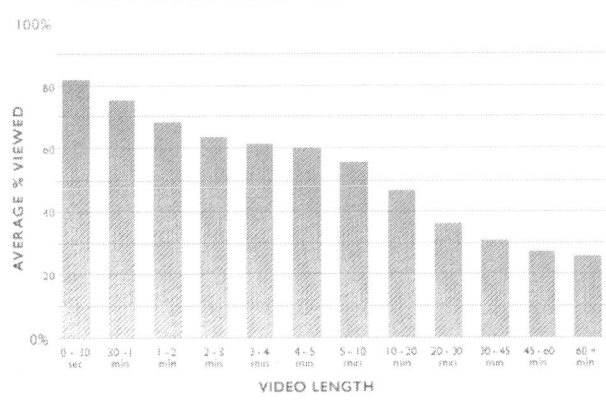

WISTIA VIDEO ANALYTICS: LENGTH MATTERS

Source: www.wistia.com

2. Follow the tried and true formula:
- Problem (Points of pain)
- Solution (Your product)
- Benefits, features

3. Make the video as high quality as possible, while staying within your budget. A video that looks good *and* tells a compelling story can create a great impression that moves customers into the sales funnel. A bad video can do more harm than good if it creates the perception the product or service is low quality.

4. Insert a call to action to wrap up the video. It could be a suggestion to visit your Website, ask for a demo, buy your product, contact you, etc. If you are going to educate, engage and/or entertain a potential customer, why not give them some encouragement to learn or do more?

How should videos be created?

There are many tools that make it easy to create different kinds of videos in-house. It comes down to the video being created and how professional it needs to be. In addition to production issues, creativity is a key consideration. These factors should be weighed to decide if making it yourself makes sense, or whether a third-party should be used. If you hire a video maker, Tony Marik, the creative director with Switch Video, says the most value comes from using someone who can offer a different perspective. "When it's your baby and its success depends on you and your ability to choose the right team and tell the story in a way that resonates well with your audience, that is a lot of stress and pressure," he says. "It is easy to cling to what you think is important and how you think things should be told and be done. This is a challenge because the entrepreneur is too close to their information. The reason you hire a third-party is they are the outsiders. All that matters is that they get what you are doing and understand what your new service does."

Lee LeFever also suggests startups let a video production

partner write the video script. "The reason you work with a third-party is they can approach it from an outsider's perspective and explain things in a way a new user might understand. If you hire someone to do the video, let them do the explaining."

CASE STUDY: A VIDEO THAT ENTERTAINS AND EDUCATES

If there is a video that illustrates the success that startups can enjoy, it is Dollar Shave Club. In September 2012, the company made a video (https://www.youtube.com/DollarShaveClub) that quickly became a viral sensation. The 94-second video, which cost $4,500 to make, featured co-founder CEO Michael Dubin walking through the company's warehouse, swinging a tennis racquet, riding a forklift, using a machete to cut tape, and dancing with a bear mascot. It was funny, irreverent and entertaining. At a time when many startups were using animated explainer videos to tell their stories, Dollar Shave Club successfully rose above the pack by being different and creative. As important, the video generated business. In the first two days after the video went live, Dollar Shave Club had 12,000 people sign up for the service. To date, the video has attracted more than 17.5 million views.

Source: https://www.youtube.com/watch?v=ZUG9qYTJMsI

CASE STUDY: THE POWER OF EXPLAINER VIDEOS

With more than 300 million users, it is difficult to believe that Dropbox once struggled to attract users. In 2008, the online storage company realized it needed something other than AdSense advertising and word-of-mouth to drive growth. The company's co-founder, Drew Houston, decided to make a four-minute video to show people how Dropbox worked. In the video world, four minutes a is long time. But Houston needed an effective way to show people why Dropbox was a better way to store online content. He decided to not only make a video but also cater it to people who used Digg, an online community in which he was personally involved. The first day after Dropbox unveiled the video, it got 70,000 new customers.

Armed with the success of using video, Houston turned to it again in 2009 when he asked Lee LeFever from Common Craft to produce a new video that would explain in a simple way what Dropbox did. Common Craft had a growing track record for creating popular explainer videos for companies such as Twitter and LinkedIn, but it was moving away from making them. After being approached by a well-known investor, Common Craft decided to make an exception with Dropbox because LeFever liked the company and how they communicated. "At the time, they had one or two million users, but I had no idea they would get hundreds of millions of users. We had a good feeling for them, which was a good sign." The result was a video - "What is Dropbox?" (http://bit.ly/1y4sXvp) that positioned the service as a "magic pocket" that would consolidate a person's files across multiple devices. "Dropbox was not that complicated of a tool, but understanding how it works in your life was a whole other thing," LeFever says. "It was not about how you use it, but why you should care about it. We talked about a guy going on a trip to Africa, and how to manage and store his videos.

> It is a tool to highlight the concept." The video was so popular (100 million views and counting) that it stayed on Dropbox's homepage for three years. LeFever says the video's longevity was interesting because Dropbox did a lot of testing to see what converted best on its homepage, and the video always topped the list.

Tool Kit

- **YouTube:** The world's most popular video-hosting service, YouTube makes it easy to share videos and create a corporate channel. It is also owned by Google, which makes it a good option for search engine optimization.
- **Vimeo:** Like YouTube, Vimeo lets users upload, share and view videos.
- **Vidyard:** A service that lets companies host and analyze their videos. It lets customers see how people are using their videos - how long they watch, the parts getting the most attention or being watched frequently.
- **Wistia:** A video hosting service that offers analytics and video marketing tools.
- **Camtasia Studio:** Tools that let you record your computer screen, and turn those recordings into professional-grade videos and screencasts.
- **iMovie:** A video production and editing software application for Mac and iOS devices.

CHAPTER 22

Leveraging Social Media to Engage

"Social media is the ultimate equalizer. It gives a voice and a platform to anyone willing to engage."

- Amy Jo Martin

Social media is enticing because many startups are enthusiastically using it. They are tweeting, updating, sharing, and posting photos, graphics and video. Why? It is about thought leadership, engagement, branding, lead generation, customer service, jockeying for competitive positioning, and even sales. But social media does not have magical powers. It can't transform a bad product into something wonderful. What social media can do, however, is amplify and promote your storytelling efforts. It can be a powerful way to make target audiences aware of what you are doing, the narratives driving your business and the products being sold. Neil Bhapkar, chief marketing officer with FlightNetwork, describes social media as "an extension of the promotion of your story; a story that lives and breathes with your company. I'm a big believer in social media being a promotion tool for your stories and content."

Getting started with social media

It is easy to fervently jump on the social media bandwagon but there are important strategic questions to ask.

1. Can social media make enough of an impact to drive brand awareness, business development, sales or customer service? And, as important, can social media be more effective in reaching these goals than other marketing channels – e.g. newsletters, a blog or videos?

2. How do target audiences conduct research and make purchase decisions using social media? Is it a key part of the buying process?

3. If social media has marketing and sales potential, what are the networks used by target audiences?

4. What are the resources (people, time) that can be allocated to social media? This will play a key role in determining the social media networks to embrace, and how active you will be. This is a key consideration given startups have limited resources. In many cases, it comes down to quality over quantity – focusing on one or a small number of social media services, rather than being everywhere.

5. How will success be defined? What metrics will be used to figure out whether social media is an effective tool within the marketing mix?

After answering these questions, you can explore the tactical options, including the specific social networks to establish a presence. Being successful social media means having a long-term commitment. It is a marathon, rather than a sprint. Doing well with social media means slogging it out on a daily basis. It is not something to focus on for a while, and then ignore when other things take priority. As well, social media success hinges on energy, engagement and creativity. While having a well-defined strategy is important, the magic happens during day-to-day operations.

There are many places to gain insight about social media tactics. Some of the leading sources include:
- Social Media Examiner (socialmediaexaminer.com)
- Social Media Today (socialmediatoday.com)
- Social Media Explorer (socialmediaexplorer.com)
- Social Mouths (socialmouths.com)
- Convince and Convert (convinceandconvert.com)

- Top Rank (toprankblog.com)
- Danny Brown (dannybrown.me)
- Razor Social (razorsocial.com/blog)

MINI-LESSON

There are two keys to social media success.

1. It is okay to walk before you run. It means tiptoeing into social media by using a smaller number of networks - e.g. Facebook and Twitter - as opposed to embracing a variety of networks at the same time. This offers the opportunity to be focused and learn, rather than being spread too thin.

2. Quality over quantity: Whatever social media network is used, it should be leveraged as well as possible. It means following best practices, engaging with target audiences, sharing good content, and monitoring performance. It is better to do one thing really well than being average or mediocre at several things.

Tool Kit

- **Hootsuite** (hootsuite.com): an online platform to publish, monitor and analyze social media activity. It also lets teams collaborate, create workflow and assign messages.
- **Sysomos** (sysomos.com): One of the leading platforms to monitor and analyze social media. It has two products: MAP, which offers unlimited queries on any topic, and Heartbeat, a cost-effective solution based on keywords.
- **Buffer** (buffercapp.com) makes it easy to manage multiple social media platforms, schedule content, collaborate with team members, and analyze activity.

- **Radian6** (radian6.com): Now owned by Saleforce.com, Radian6 lets you track, monitor and publish social media activity.
- **Buzzsumo** (buzzsumo.com) lets you see if your company has been mentioned and how many times that content has been shared on different social networks.

CHAPTER 23

Jump-Start Your Marketing With Blogging

"Blogging and the Internet allow us to engage in a lot more real time conversations as opposed to a one-way dump of information or a message."
- **Indra Nooyi**

As a storytelling platform, blogs are a powerful way to accomplish multiple objectives: establish thought leadership, demonstrate industry insight, and deliver corporate updates. As a bonus, search engines love blogs that are regularly updated with fresh content. These benefits make blogs appealing to startups seeking a cost-effective way to drive their marketing and sales.

Randy Frisch, chief operating officer with Uberflip, a content marketing company, says blogs are an easy way for a startup to embrace storytelling and content marketing. "They offer the least resistance and the least amount of excuses to get started. You need a video camera and editing skills to make a half decent video. You need a graphic designer for an infographic. For a blog, all you need is a notepad and some tools to make sure you are optimizing it for SEO."

But blogging is also a crowded landscape. While it is difficult to determine exactly how many blogs exist, WordPress.com hosts 75.3 million blogs in more than 120 languages, and 100,000 new blogs are created every day. That is a lot of competition, so you need to be creative, focused and pro-active to stand out from the crowd.

Once you are convinced a blog can be a good storytelling vehicle, here is how to get started:

1. Establish an editorial focus: It is easier to create engaging content by focusing on a particular topic or market. This also makes it easy for readers to know what they are going to get when reading your blog. Another key is deciding how many posts to write each week. For some startups, one post is enough, while other startups will write five posts a week. The number of posts depends on resources (people) and the value your content delivers. I would recommend starting with fewer posts so everyone involved is comfortable and a rhythm can be established. At some point, the time could be right to do more posts.

2. Define your goals: Be clear about objectives and how success is defined. For some startups, a blog is about driving brand awareness. Startups with traction may want to use a blog to drive thought leadership to better position themselves within the competitive landscape. For some startups, blogging can be a powerful inbound marketing tool because their content is high quality and interesting. Two good examples are Buffer (https://blog.bufferapp.com/), which does insightful posts on social media, and Wistia, a video hosting analytics service, which creates excellent videos on how to make videos (http://wistia.com/blog).

3. Determine who will write the blog: This is a critical ingredient – no writers = no blog posts. It is important to identify if there are people internally who can write posts, or whether external resources (e.g. freelancers, contractors, agencies) need to be hired. A key part of this decision will be how many posts will be written. If there is only one post a week, this job can easily be done internally.

4. Create an editorial calendar so it is clear to everyone who will be writing blog posts and when they need to be created, edited and published. An editorial calendar, which can be a spreadsheet, can also include key events – conferences, holidays, etc. – to drive theme-based posts.

5. Start writing blog posts: Here is a list of key ingredients:

- Create a snappy or eye-catching headline that triggers a strong emotional reaction or response.
- Write 350 to 600 words; not enough words suggest the post has no substance, while too many words seems like a lot of work.
- Use images, graphics or video to make posts more accessible and interesting.
- Insert links to relevant content, including third-party content. It is about delivering value.
- Make it easy for people to share content on social media by offering user-friendly tools or widgets.
- Allow people to leave comments. Comments can be moderated to make sure they are not spam or offensive.
- Promote blog posts on social media, newsletters, email, etc.

How to generate blog ideas

Armed with an editorial focus and a good grasp on how to meet the needs of target audiences, it is easier to come up with ideas for blog posts. Ideas are the fuel that makes blogging work so they need to be captured in a structured way. As important, you need to rank blog ideas as they materialize. Some ideas will be great blog material, while others have potential but need time to get them in better shape.

One of the best (and most interesting) ways to develop blog post ideas is Marcus Sheridan's company-wide brainstorming approach. Sheridan (a content marketing consultant also known as *"The Sales Lion"*) says companies should gather employees in a room - senior executives, sales and marketing teams, customer support, admin staff, etc. With different perspectives and experience at the table, Sheridan says it should be a snap to get at least 100 ideas by collecting the questions asked by a company's customers. It is a simple, but brilliant, approach when you think about the number of questions asked by customers. Your customer service people, for example, may get questions never experienced by the sales or marketing teams, and vice versa. Marcus says 100 ideas for blog posts is equivalent to having a year's worth of content based on writing two posts a week.

Even without a company-wide brainstorming session, it is important to get blog post ideas from everyone. Truth be told, the most challenging part about writing a blog on a regular basis is having enough content to keep it going. Tapping into the collective knowledge of your employees is a great tool to jump-start the process. Another way to keep the blog engine rumbling is having multiple authors. This makes it easier to create blog posts and, as important, it gives the blog a variety of ideas and perspectives. You may also want to consider inviting people from outside the company to write guest posts.

Content Idea/Writing Tools:

- Portent Content Idea Generator: (http://www.portent.com/tools/title-maker) Type in a keyword to get topic ideas for content.
- RYP Content Idea Generator: (http://www.rypmarketing.com/tools/topics/): Type in a keyword to brainstorm content topics.
- Atomic Reach (www.atomicreach.com): a free tool that helps improve the quality of your writing.
- HubSpot Bug Topic Generator (http://www.hubspot.com/blog-topic-generator): Generate ideas for blog posts in seconds by entering a few nouns.

- CoSchedule Headline Analyzer: A free tool to see if your headline has what it takes to be noticed (coschedule.com/headline-analyzer)
- Editorial Calendar: A free WordPress plug-in that makes it easy to schedule blog posts (wordpress.org/plugins/editorial-calendar/)

Best practices for blogging success:

1. Be customer-centric: As a "publisher", you need to think about what people want to read as opposed to what you want them to read. It may not seem like a big difference, but many startups stumble because they believe a blog is a glorified brochure to talk about their products, people and events. If a blog is self-serving, it does not take long before "blog fatigue" sets in. A better approach is being customer-centric, which means thinking about the different ways a blog can deliver value on a consistent basis. What are the trends, news or tools that people find interesting or want to learn about? How can your insight and experience give people a new way of looking at things?

Mark Hayes, director of communications with Shopify, which has one of the world's most popular e-commerce blogs, said the formula he applies to writing blog posts is a split between research and preparation, and writing and promotion. "Way too many people spend the vast majority of their time writing the blog post," he says. "You need to do research and make sure you are writing about the right topic and talking to the right influencers."

2. Don't assume people will magically discover your blog posts. After writing posts, they need to be promoted - be it on social media (Twitter, Facebook, LinkedIn, etc.), newsletters and your Website. It is also important to "seed" blog posts by sharing them on places where content is aggregated. Some of the more popular places include Reddit, Facebook, Stumbleupon, Digg and Hacker News. If you are writing about digital marketing, for example, it makes sense to share posts on Inbound.org or Growthhackers.com so a wider audience can discover them. It also helps to market the blog by inserting the link into email signatures, business cards and marketing and sales collateral.

Shopify's Mark Hayes said there are several "hacks" that can be used to promote a new blog post.

After a new post is published, his team inserts the link into old posts focused on the same topic. This provides the new post with in-bound links, which are a key factor for search engine rankings.

Shopify also sends tweets to people who might be interested in the blog post. This captures the attention of people who might have otherwise not noticed the blog post.

When writing a blog post, Shopify looks to see if there are ways it can insert expert commentary. This increases the likelihood these experts will promote the blog post.

"No piece of content we create should rely on our existing audience to be successful…ever," Hayes says. "Every piece of content needs to drive its own new audience. I tell my people that if you publish something, it should be successful, even if Shopify does not post it on Twitter or Facebook, or it goes on our newsletter. When it comes to promotion, you can't publish and pray. You publish a blog post at 10 a.m. and then you spend the rest of the day and the day after promoting the hell out of it."

3. Be an engaged member of the community. Within your blog posts, quote, cite and link to other blogs offering different perspective or ideas. Many of the best blog posts are written in reaction to what someone else has published. Creating a dialogue is a powerful part of blogging. Another best practice is adding insight and context by commenting on the blogs of other people and organizations. Bloggers like comments because it means their work is generating a reaction.

4. Measure, measure, measure. It is important to see how each post performs. How many times did people read it? How many links did they click on? How many comments were left? How often was it shared on social media? Some of the tools to measure performance include Google Analytics, Chartbeat, Woopra and Clicky.

Content Publishing Tools:

- WordPress: (www.wordpress.org) the world's leading content management platform used to power blog and Websites.
- Tumblr: (www.tumblr.com): A micro-blogging platform and social media platform now owned by Yahoo!
- Blogger: (www.blogger.com): A free blog publishing tool owned by Google.
- Ghost: Bills itself as a distraction-free blogging platform. Free if you host it; paid plans start at $10.

CHAPTER 24

Tapping Into the Popularity of Infographics

"Infographics' are a trend. It may eventually fade away, though I don't see it happening over the next five years. But a thing that will stay here forever is the need for data visualization."
- Uldis Leifert

In the past few years, infographics have become popular as brands look for new ways to engage and educate target audiences. Infographics, which use a combination of text, graphic design and illustrations, are user-friendly while delivering lots of information. Infographics are a great way to talk about your company or product, or interesting industry trends. With creativity and good ideas, an infographic can pack a punch and attract a lot of attention. Even better, people seem to have an insatiable appetite for infographics, so using them as storytelling vehicles plays into a market with lots of demand and interest. Another positive about infographics is they have become less expensive to create. There are a number of do-it-yourself online services such as Piktochart, Easel.ly and Venngage that make it easy to develop an infographic.

Best practices:

1. Leverage a good story by tapping into interesting ideas and eye-catching facts or data. An infographic is a visual, engaging story that can be easily consumed. An infographic does not have to be complicated or overwhelm people with facts or information. It probably goes without saying an infographic should serve the needs of your target audiences. What are their interests, or the things they need to know? There is no lack of stories to tell using an infographic, but incorporating statistics and numbers tends to resonate best.

So, how do you come up with killer ideas for infographics? One of the best approaches is brainstorming with employees. What are the questions being asked by customers? What are the interesting trends that your employees have seen, or statistics that have caught their attention? Infographic ideas can also come from doing keyword research to discover insight into how people are finding you or your competitors. Tools such as Buzzsumo or Google Keyword Planner can provide valuable insight.

Shawn Arora, founder of Launchspark Video, which creates video and infographics, said brainstorming works well by thinking about how you would explain a concept to a friend or colleague. "Getting from strategy to story is more art than science," he says. "At this step, it's important to brainstorm topics that have one clear theme per idea, and focuses on a clear benefit to your customer."

2. Create a storyboard to provide the story with shape and a rough structure. Think of an infographic as a series of scenes in a play or movie with leading characters. There should be a natural flow between each scene. A storyboard also sets the stage for design. You can create a storyboard by mapping it out on paper (old school!), software such as Draw.io, Toon Boom Animation and Storyboard That, or mockup tools such as Balsamiq, Mockingbird or HotGloo. You want to turn ideas into tangible concepts that guide the infographic's production.

3. Embrace a user-friendly design: You want an infographic to be a snap to consume, even though it may contain a lot of information. It involves the use of interesting or attractive graphics and just enough text to explain the ideas or facts. The better the design, the more attention it will receive and the more it will be shared. Many online infographic services offer free and premium priced templates to capitalize on user-friendly designs.

4. Like any kind of content, do not assume creating an infographic will cause people to beat a path to your door. You need to publish it in multiple places and make it easy to share

on social media or embed on a Website. An infographic can appear on a landing page that can be used to collect information from people who want more information about what your company does. It can be embedded in a blog post or within a presentation, or shared on Slideshare.org. To drive distribution, provide easy ways to share an infographic on social media or embed it on Websites. Another option is submitting infographics to places such as Visual.ly, and offering them to blogs and news sites looking for interesting content.

Here are two examples of startups that have successfully used infographics to drive their marketing and sales efforts:

This infographic by Uberflip looks at the content marketing landscape.

The State of Content Marketing
ADOPTION, TACTICS & RESULTS IN 2014

Content marketing — every marketer talks about it and more than half of companies are already consistently producing content. But what exactly are they doing? Which tactics are they relying on? Are they seeing results? What does the future hold? Take a look!

A DOMINATING TREND

In just a few years, content marketing has become a priority for most companies, to the point that content tactics are already claiming an average of 39% of their total ad/marketing budget.

Uberflip: http://hub.uberflip.com/h/i/19271195-the-state-of-content-marketing-in-2014-infographic

STORYTELLING FOR STARTUPS 235

This infographic created by RateHub, an online service to compare mortgages offers user-friendly industry insight about the mortgage market.

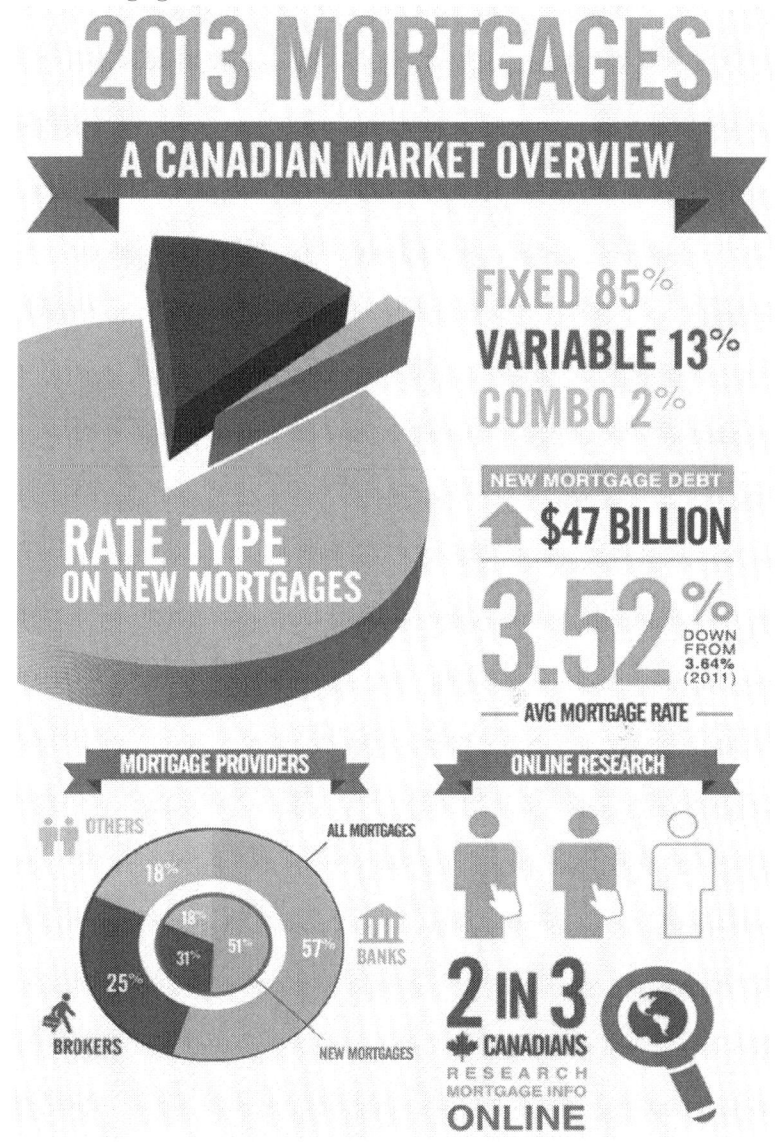

2013 MORTGAGES
A CANADIAN MARKET OVERVIEW

RATE TYPE ON NEW MORTGAGES
- FIXED 85%
- VARIABLE 13%
- COMBO 2%

NEW MORTGAGE DEBT
↑ $47 BILLION

AVG MORTGAGE RATE
3.52% DOWN FROM 3.64% (2011)

MORTGAGE PROVIDERS

ALL MORTGAGES:
- OTHERS 18%
- BANKS 57%
- BROKERS 25%

NEW MORTGAGES:
- 18%
- 51%
- 31%

ONLINE RESEARCH

2 IN 3 CANADIANS RESEARCH MORTGAGE INFO ONLINE

Source: www.ratehub.ca/blog/2013/05/2013-mortgages-a-canadian-market-overview-infographic/

Tool Kit

- **Canva:** An online platform that makes it easy to create a variety of graphics and icons for Websites, blogs, social media and presentations. (canva.com)
- **Easel.ly** features thousands of free infographic templates and design objects. (easel.ly)
- **Infogr.am** makes it easy to create infographics and charts. (infogr.am)
- **Venngage** makes it a snap to create and publish infographics by offering templates, maps and icons. (venngage.com)
- **Piktochart:** A user-friendly online tool to make infographics. It features templates and the ability to build infographics from scratch (piktochart.com)

CHAPTER 25
Creating White Papers That Have Sizzle

"White papers remain effective because they combine the persuasiveness of an article with the product information of a brochure. They educate without selling."
- Ryan Malone

When most people think about white papers (assuming they think of white papers at all!), they likely see them as boring, bland and inaccessible. To be fair, it is not inaccurate given most white papers are bland, boring and inaccessible! A key part of the white paper's low regard may have to do with the fact it was the child of government policy, going back to 1922 when the U.K. government published the Churchill White Paper.

But do not write off white papers because most companies stumble and fumble the ball by insisting on sticking with the old ways of creating them. Instead, think about white papers as an opportunity to provide thought leadership, while leveraging creativity, good writing and design panache. As we have mentioned throughout the book, it helps to take a customer-centric view. You want people to be engaged, while delivering well-researched information about an industry trend, topic or opportunity. White papers should be accessible, not something people slog through because they are a necessary evil. (Note: I group e-books into the white paper category. In many ways, they follow the same format.)

For startups, white papers demonstrate domain expertise through content that educates and engages. You want people to see your startup in a new or different light. The biggest benefits of white papers include:

- Establishing thought leadership
- Lead generation and sales
- Educating potential customers.
- Growing an email newsletter list
- Fueling social media activity

Best practices:

1. White papers do not have to be long – 750 to 2,500 words is enough content to achieve your goals: education, engagement and, maybe, entertainment. When a white paper is too long, it seems like too much work to read, even if it has high-quality content. Another key ingredient is good writing that inspires, motivates and gets people thinking. The traditional take on a white paper is they are dull as molasses, but this formula is dead in the water given the fast-paced, instant gratification digital world.

2. Tell, don't sell. White papers are not sales collateral. Well, they are sales collateral but certainly not you-need-to-buy-now collateral. Instead, white papers should meet the interests of people looking to learn more about a particular subject, trend or technology. A white paper has to be authentic, focused and designed to educate rather than sell.

3. If appropriate and relevant, include your clients in the white paper. Use them to illuminate your thoughts and provide tangible, real-world case studies. It is a good way to strengthen relationships with customers by showing that you value their business.

4. Good design is a must-have. Ever read a white paper with a wall of text? Ever want to read a wall of text? Top-notch design makes anything, including white papers, more accessible. By using charts, graphics, photos and pull quotes, the sea of text disappears. Instead, there are well-defined and user-friendly sections.

5. To extract value from a white paper, create landing pages that offer a taste of the content. If someone wants to download the white paper, they have to provide their name and email address – a small price for valuable content. This creates a win-win scenario that delivers insight to the reader, and marketing and sales opportunities to your startup.

6. Leverage analytics: To drive marketing and sales activities, you want to know how many people downloaded a white paper, how many times they opened it, how much time they spent reading it, and how many links were clicked. Using a service such as Uberflip can offer lots of valuable data.

Christina O'Reilly, ex-director of marketing with 360incentives, says white papers are slowly being approached in new ways. "White papers are the last of the marketing tools to have been updated given the way we now consume and deliver information. If you look at infographics and email, they leverage visual aids; we are starting to see that with white papers. Our white papers are more visual, use images and larger headlines."

O'Reilly says white papers played an important role in establishing 360incentives as thought leaders in the incentives and consumer rebate world. She credits the company's success to having an in-house writer, who can transform ideas into drafts, and a graphics team that can make white papers visually compelling. "It is our opportunity to look at it differently," she says. "At the end of the day, a white paper is about positioning that will separate you from the competition. O'Reilly adds that white paper content can be re-purposed to become the basis for a Webinar, a blog post, infographic or video. Here is an example of how 360incentives uses design, different colours and font sizes, quotes and charts to make its white papers more accessible.

LEVERAGING THE CONSUMER REBATE

Considering Promoting Your Brand With A Rebate Program? Follow These Steps to Create Happy Customers Who Can Out-Market Your Entire Marketing Team!

CUSTOMERS WHO CAN OUT-MARKET YOUR MARKETING TEAM?

Does this sound crazy? As a marketing professional, you are no doubt already aware of the sweeping changes in what factors most influence consumer choices these days. The numbers for social proof are probably even higher now, but according to this 2009 study by The Nielsen Company, the greatest form of influence on a customer's buying decision is social proof or *"recommendations from people known."*

HAVE SOME DEGREE OF TRUST* IN THE FOLLOWING FORMS OF ADVERTISING
APRIL 2009

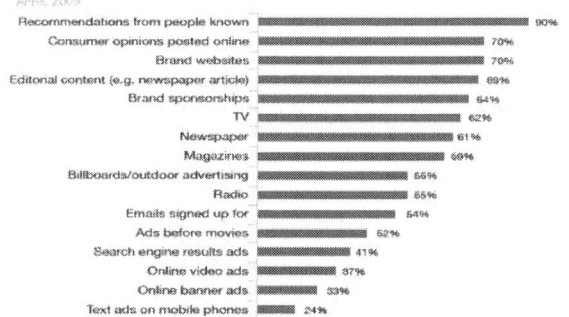

Form of Advertising	%
Recommendations from people known	90%
Consumer opinions posted online	70%
Brand websites	70%
Editorial content (e.g. newspaper article)	69%
Brand sponsorships	64%
TV	62%
Newspaper	61%
Magazines	59%
Billboards/outdoor advertising	55%
Radio	55%
Emails signed up for	54%
Ads before movies	52%
Search engine results ads	41%
Online video ads	37%
Online banner ads	33%
Text ads on mobile phones	24%

SOURCE: THE NIELSEN COMPANY

Source: www.360incentives.com

Tool Kit

- **Uberflip:** an online platform that lets brands aggregate social content, blog posts and content such as white papers, e-books and video in a user-friendly digital hub (uberflip.com)
- **LookBookHQ:** A tool for marketers that lets them present content and calls to action, as well as leverage analytics (lookbookhq.com)
- **Pressly:** A user-friendly way to curate internal and third party content into a hub that can be displayed on Websites and email newsletters. (pressly.com)

CHAPTER 26

Email Newsletters that Get Read

"Your email inbox is a bit like a Las Vegas roulette machine. You know, you just check it and check it, and every once in a while there's some juicy little tidbit of reward."
— **Douglas Rushkoff**

When it comes to email, it would be fair to say people are obsessed with controlling their inbox. Given this battle, you would think that trying to send them email newsletters would be a huge challenge. Surprisingly, this is not the case. Email newsletters are becoming one of the most effective digital marketing tools. For example, a global study by Quartz about news consumption discovered that executives use email newsletters as their primary news source. So why are newsletters appealing? For consumers, it is an expedient way to receive interesting content. For startups, it is an engaging and inexpensive way to develop an ongoing and long-term relationship by offering valuable information. The best newsletters have content about a startup's products, but they also provide insight and information about industry trends and news, as well as a selection of third-party content.

When using newsletters as a marketing tool, here are some guiding principles:

1. It needs to be customer-centric, not product-centric. If someone is going to let another email into their inbox, it has to meet their interests. A newsletter that only highlights a company's products will encourage someone to click on "unsubscribe".

2. There needs to be insight and information on how customers can learn, improve and grow. It is about delivering ideas and news-you-can-use, rather than selling a product.

3. Sharing relevant third-party content shows a willingness to expose people to more ideas. This is akin to inserting external links into blog posts. Sending people to another Website makes your content more valuable.

4. Make it easy for people to share the newsletter and its content. As startups look to expand brand awareness and their digital footprint, the ability to spread the word is a must-have.

The tactical creation of newsletters is fairly straightforward. Like any content, there has to be a strategic and tactical plan to address issues such as:
- An editorial focus and the kind of content to feature.
- A publishing schedule – e.g. daily, weekly or monthly – based on the interests of target audiences. Most startups will publish on a monthly basis.
- Identifying the people responsible for creating content - writers, editors and designers.
- Selecting a publishing platform. The most popular include services such as MailChimp, AWeber and Constant Contact.
- Creating user-friendly ways for people to subscribe to the newsletter such as a sign up box on your Website.

From a best practices perspective, Freshbooks, an online invoicing service, used to publish a newsletter that had the right editorial mix. The newsletter (see below) was divided into three sections. The biggest chunk was devoted to putting the spotlight on the company's customers. Using text, photos and/or videos, it had stories about how customers were successfully using Freshbooks to run their businesses. While the product was featured, the newsletter was a vehicle to inspire existing and potential customers. The other sections, which used less real estate, had information about events that Freshbooks was attending, product updates, and some blog content.

Source: www.freshbooks.com

Moz, which offers search engine and content marketing tools, also publishes a popular newsletter that features 10 links, many of them from external sources. The newsletter's strengths include good design and a variety of content that make it user-friendly and, as important, a solid sales and marketing tool.

The Moz Top 10

Can you believe the year is almost over? Don't let your brain check out for the holidays just yet. This week we have news for you about how Google sees the future of mobile search, the detailed info you need to know about Panda 4.1, and a guide to generating rich snippets. Here's the Moz Top 10, your chance to get a leg up on those SERPS while everyone else you know is waiting in line at the airport.

1. Micro Data & Schema.org Rich Snippets: Everything You Need to Know
The team over at Builtvisible recently updated this amazing guide. Learn everything you need to know from what micro data is to how to create interactive breadcrumbs.

2. OMG! Mobile Voice Survey Reveals Teens Love to Talk
Google shares their data about who's searching for what and how. Find out what kinds of queries you should be anticipating.

3. Google's Gary Illyes Discusses Mobile as a Ranking Factor
Speaking of mobile, Eric Enge gets Gary Illyes to open up about mobile, SSL, and what the future may hold for Penguin.

4. Panda 4.1 Google Leaked Dos and Don'ts - Whiteboard Friday
Josh Bachynski delivers the inside information about what you should (and should not) be doing to Panda-proof your site..

5. Introducing The Simple SEO Site Audit Tool
Bill Sebald shares Sean Malseed's tool so you can make sure you have all the right schema in all the right places.

Source: www.moz.com

Tool Kit

- **Mailchimp:** One of the most popular email newsletter services. It has a large library of templates. Free for up to 2,000 subscribers; paid plans start at $10/month (mailchimp.com)
- **AWeber:** A full-featured platform with a drag-and-drop editor, subscriber segmenting based on their actions, and analytics. It integrates into WordPress, Facebook and PayPal. (aweber.com)
- **Constant Contact:** an email publishing and distribution tool that makes it easy to create email newsletters (constantcontact.com)
- **Mad Mimi:** Positioned as the "easiest email ever", it lets you create, send, share and track email newsletters. (madmimi.com)

CHAPTER 27

The Press Release is Alive and Well

"If you are planning on using either of the following phrases in your press release: "We are thrilled," or "we are excited," I have three words for you: Throw it away."
– John Sternal

For years, press releases were corporate staples. When a company had news, it issued a press release. Today, press releases seem old school. It makes you wonder why press releases still exist given the new options. While press releases are not top of mind these days when it comes to storytelling and marketing, it does not mean press releases are irrelevant. At the right time or place, press releases can play a solid role. "I think press releases are important because they tell the world what we think is newsworthy," says Mark Organ, CEO and co-founder with Influitive, an influencer marketing company. "Because fewer companies are using press releases, it can be a way to cut through the noise."

How do press releases fit into the storytelling landscape?

In many ways, press releases are like the marks on the wall that show a child's growth. Each mark symbolizes progress for the world to see. For startups, press releases are a public way to show the proverbial ball is moving forward. Not every press release has to be exciting and dramatic (just as not every mark on the wall has to be several inches higher than the last!), but they demonstrate all-important traction. I like to think about press releases as stories with a specific format and structure. They do not need to ooze with flair because, at best, press releases are low-key vehicles that offer options to get more details. Here are some ideas on how to create press releases with a better chance of being read:
 1. Identify the story you want to tell. It could be a new product release, the hiring of a key executive, winning an industry award, raising venture capital, or achieving an important milestone (e.g. 10,000 customers).

2. Select the target audiences. Who do you want to reach and what are the goals and objectives – news coverage, brand awareness, inbound links, etc.?

3. Write a press release using a story structure, and six to 10 paragraphs. Begin with the news or the key idea to highlight. Then, offer some context – why is the news important or interesting? Next, provide details about the story, along with a quote that adds flavour.

4. Set the stage to drive more interest by providing contact information (name, telephone number, email address), and links to other content such as videos and photos.

5. Decide whether to publicize the press release using a wire service for extensive distribution, or share it via social media and free online services.

In many ways, a press release is a "teaser" to attract attention. It does not have to be long or packed with details; it just needs to generate enough interest to encourage people to learn more.

Here are some best practices to consider:

1. **Be strategic about press releases.** Think of them as ingrained part of your storytelling machine. Ideally, they are created on a regular basis (e.g. weekly, bi-weekly or monthly) so they become part of how the business operates. As important, everyone will begin to recognize press release opportunities.

2. Develop a target list of the reporters and bloggers you want to reach. Create a spreadsheet with the following fields: name, title, email address, Website, social media (Twitter,

LinkedIn), interests and relevant articles. Enter new sources as you read blog posts and news articles, attend conferences, or wade through social media.

3. Recognize there are internal and external press releases. Some press releases are created with little fanfare. They are published on your Website, and distributed via social media. Then, there are more newsworthy press releases (e.g. high-profile customer wins, awards, financings, etc.) that merit distribution on a news wire service. Using a wire service costs money but offers opportunities for media coverage.

4. Press releases should be short and sweet. A press release of 400 to 750 words is enough copy to tell a story and provide background information. In today's world, reporters and bloggers are time-strapped so you need to provide the relevant details quickly. A press release is more a taste than a full meal.

CASE STUDY: A DIFFERENT KIND OF PRESS RELEASE

When Microsoft acquired Mojang, the makers of the popular game, Minecraft, for $2.5-billion in September 2014, it came as a major surprise for a variety of reasons: the fact that Microsoft, the world's largest software maker, was the buyer, the size of the deal, and why the deal happened. Mojang could have easily issued a standard press release about the deal. Instead, Owen Hill, Mojang's Chief Word Officer (yes, that is a real title), wrote a press release on the company's blog (https://mojang.com/2014/09/yes-were-being-bought-by-microsoft/) that broke away from the traditional format. It answered many of the key questions about the deal, but also conceded there was uncertainly about Microsoft's plans for Minecraft.

The takeaway is press releases do not have to be boring vehicles that follow a standard template - statement, statement, quote, statement. Instead, press releases can be creative, conversational and informal, as long as they tell a story and answer the key questions. If a startup such as Mojang has a particular culture or distinct community, it could be a no-brainer to use language that is different and authentic, rather than conventional.

Tool Kit

- **Pitch Engine:** an online service to create and share press releases (www.pitchengine.com)
- **MarketWired:** a press release distribution service (www.marketwired.com)
- **Instant Press Release:** a free online tool to quickly create press releases (http://www.ducttapemarketing.com/instant-press-release)
- **Pr.co:** Create press releases and an online pressroom that includes a press kit and clippings. (www.pr.co)

CHAPTER 28

Going Against the Grain with Podcasting

"Podcasting is great. Total freedom."
- Bill Burr

While I was writing this book, podcasts were not part of the original plan. After they became popular (along with blogs) around 2005/2006, podcasts began to fade into the background - probably because video became easier to create and distribute via services such as YouTube. But podcasts are making a comeback. The question is "why?" It may have to do with the strength of audio broadcasts within the media landscape. While the Web has disrupted television and music, traditional radio continues to survive and thrive. At the same time, podcasts have benefited from the popularity of well-produced shows such as *"Serial"* (more than five million downloads and counting). Another factor is how services such as Blubrry, LibSyn and iTunes have made podcasts much easier to create and distribute.

Podcasts can also be seen as a storytelling medium that goes against the grain. While brands have enthusiastically embraced social media, content marketing and video, there is not an over-saturation of podcasts or intense competition. When you combine the popularity of audio broadcasts and a less noisy podcasting landscape, it offers good opportunities to capture the spotlight.

Leesa Renee Hall, a podcaster and the *"Money Talk Lady"*, says successful podcasts embrace the following best practices:

- Decide on a format. It could be interviews with customers or industry experts, tutorials on how to use products, or a talk show between two or more people.
- Be flexible about the length. Hall says the audience will tell you if a podcast is too short or too long. "As long as you can get your point across without repeating yourself, the length shouldn't be determined by you, the producer, but by the audience."
- Create an RSS feed so the podcast can be syndicated through services such as iTunes and Stitcher (stitcher.com).

- Create video and audio versions of a podcast. The video can be used for desktop or laptop audiences, while audio can be accessed on mobile devices or while driving.

CASE STUDY: FOLLOWING A STARTUP'S JOURNEY

There are few startups using podcasts, but that could change as podcasting comes back into vogue. If startups do embrace podcasting, one of the leading reasons could be *"StartUp"*, a podcast created by Alex Blumberg, a radio producer for NPR's *"This American Life"* and the co-founder of *"Planet Money"*. When Blumberg and co-founder Matt Lieber decided to develop a podcast network, Gimlet Media, Blumberg decided to chronicle his journey through, what else, podcasts (http://gimletmedia.com/show/startup/). The episodes feature everything from investor pitches, arguments with his wife, and negotiations with Lieber. While it is left to be seen whether Gimlet becomes a vibrant business, the podcasts have attracted a wide audience and the company has raised $1.5-million in venture capital.

Tool Kit:
- **Blubrry :** A one-stop destination for podcasting software and services (www.blubrry.com)
- **LibSyn:** One of the most popular places to host and distribute podcasts (www.libsyn.com/)
- **Call Record for Skype:** Easily record interviews for podcasts using Skype (www.ecamm.com/mac/callrecorder/)

- **Adobe Audition:** Record, edit and create audit content (creative.adobe.com/products/audition)
- **ID3 Editor:** Add and edit attributes for ID3 tags (www.pa-software.com/id3editor/)
- **Audacity:** A free, open-source platform for recording and editing audio (audacity.sourceforge.net/)

KEY TAKEAWAY:

Creating high-quality content is a combination of art and science, but it helps to have a structured approach that harnesses creativity and discipline.

"Be so good they can't ignore you." - Steve Martin, comedian/actor

KEY QUESTIONS:

1. Who are your target audiences?

2. What kind of stories do they consume?

3. Who is going to create your content?

4. How are you going to measure content success?

5. What kind of content is the competition producing?

CHAPTER 29
Telling Stories to Live Audiences

"For me, conferences are like little mental vacations: a chance to go visit an interesting place for a couple of days, and come back rested and refreshed with new ideas and perspectives."
- Erin McKean

Since Chapter 19, we have been talking about a variety of storytelling channels. All of them have been digital, which is the major focus for many startups because it is how a growing number of consumers get information. But there are many non-digital places to tell stories. One of the most compelling is a conference where entrepreneurs can tell a story to a live audience. As someone who organized conferences (mesh and meshmarketing) and who has spoken at many conferences, there is something powerful about speaking at a conference. My personal belief is people, for whatever reason, take you more seriously if you have been invited to give a keynote, speak on a panel or do a workshop. There is an aura; you must be smart enough to deserve to speak in public.

Truth be told, the reality is different. Behind the scenes, conferences are, in many ways, about organizers scrambling to arrange speakers so they can sell tickets and sponsorship packages. While keynote speakers are carefully selected, many panels receive less attention from organizers. This, however, is how entrepreneurs can discover new places to tell their stories. Here is a game plan for pursuing conference speaking opportunities:

1. Start by researching the conferences where you want to speak. It could be high profile conferences attended by many people, or small events focused on your industry or niche. The more focused and relevant, the more likely it is the right speaking opportunity.
2. Look at how each conference handles speakers. Some conferences have an open call for speakers where you submit an expression of interest. Some conferences are by invite-only. Some conferences are pay-per-play; if you sponsor the conference, you get a speaking slot. How you approach conference organizers depends on your budget and interest in speaking.

3. In pursuing conference organizers who are open to submissions, there are two best practices.
    - After researching a conference's focus and the type of speakers invited to attend, pitch yourself as someone who can offer relevant industry expertise and insight. As well, provide details about why you would be a good speaker (e.g. links to videos), and demonstrate a willingness to promote the event. If you have thousands of Twitter followers, that is a good marketing tool.
    - To make life even easier for an organizer, submit a "package" that involves a panel topic or idea, and several other panelists. For many organizers, this can be a gift because it means less work.
4. Start your preparations for conferences at least three to six months in advice, perhaps longer for popular conferences.

Like anything, speaking at conferences involves preparation and work. It could mean working your way up the ladder by initially speaking at small local events such as meet-ups and demo days. This lets you gain more experience and work on a story that audiences find interesting and engaging. As you speak at more conferences, your profile can expand. This makes it easier for conference organizers to discover you, and/or provides more credibility when seeking speaking opportunities.

KEY TAKEAWAY:

Speaking at conferences is a great way to build a personal and brand profile. You need a plan of attack that involves doing research to identify and pursue the best opportunities.

"It usually takes me more than three weeks to prepare a good impromptu speech." - Mark Twain

KEY QUESTIONS:

1. What conferences do you want to speak at?

2. Why are these conferences particularly attractive?

3. What topics will you want to talk about?

4. How can you get conference experience?

5. How do you need to prepare for speaking opportunities?

EXERCISE:

Identify the conferences where you want to pursue a speaking opportunity. Learn how speakers are selected and how far in advance you need to express an interest in speaking, or make a submission.

CONCLUSION

"Over the years, I have become convinced that we learn best—and change—from hearing stories that strike a chord within us. Those in leadership positions who fail to grasp or use the power of stories risk failure for their companies and for themselves."
- John Kotter, Harvard Business School professor

There has never been a better time for story-driven marketing and good storytelling.

To stand out from the crowd and establish your startup as an industry leader, you need to embrace the power of storytelling. Storytelling is a key part of how startups need to operate. It is an attitude, strategy and tactical approach that can be developed and nurtured through commitment, practice, experimentation and an eagerness to explore new ideas and concepts. It is a willingness to make mistakes because failure is sometimes the path to success. As important, a large marketing budget is not needed for good storytelling. Instead, storytelling needs healthy doses of creativity, agility and focus.

One of the most important things about story-driven marketing is it is a fluid, ongoing process - a marathon rather than a sprint. It can take time for a startup to find its storytelling groove because it is new behavior and activity that requires a different approach strategically and tactically. Some of the best storytellers such Moz.com and HubSpot had humble beginnings. Many companies began modestly with a good Website and an active blog.

As they gained traction, their storytelling "portfolios" slowly began to expand, fuelled by a growing audience that generated more business opportunities. The key lesson is every journey begins with a single step. It could take awhile to become a good storyteller but you have to start somewhere. Storytelling is one of the best ways to support and accelerate growth - and it can be a lot of fun because stories inspire, excite, motivate and drive your business forward.

The biggest takeaway from this book is how story-driven marketing has become a competitive necessity. At a time when consumers are time-strapped and multi-tasking (not really paying attention), storytelling is the vehicle to make them stop and take notice - not an easy task. The ability to capture someone's attention is a powerful proposition. It lets companies put the spotlight on the value of their products and get people engaged so they can become customers and advocates. In a noisy and busy world, storytelling has become a powerful tool to carve out a competitive edge.

Given the potential of storytelling, companies of all shapes and sizes have to jump on the bandwagon. As I said in the opening chapter: "Companies that tell great stories, win. Companies that don't, lose." The world is moving too fast, innovation is happening at a rapid-fire pace, and the ability to effectively deliver information is becoming more difficult. The "killer app" to get in front of consumers is story-driven marketing. End of story. For brands already telling stories, this book has worked if it offers more insight about how to do things better or differently. For brands new to storytelling, this book has done its job if you decide that storytelling is a must-do activity.

Finally, let's take a look at the key parts of becoming a good storyteller:
- Recognize the benefits and value that storytelling plays in helping startups establish a clear sense of what they do, how their product delivers value, and who they serve.
- Create a "core story" that forms the foundation for all the places where stories will be told.
- Identify target audiences so your stories are told in the right places at the right time.
- Establish a strategic plan that prioritizes the stories that will deliver bang for the buck to achieve your goals.
- Leverage your best storytellers – internal and external players such as freelancers, consultants and agencies.
- When creating stories, follow best practices that always include taking a customer-centric approach.

The time is now to tell stories!

READING LIST

Content Strategy for the Web
Kristina Halvorson, Melissa Rich
http://contentstrategy.com/

Influence Marketing
Danny Brown, Sam Fiorella
http://influencemarketingbook.com/

Simplicity
Bill Jensen
http://www.simplerwork.com/

Feed the Startup Beast
Drew Williams, Jonathan Verney
http://feedthebeast.biz/

The Inside Advantage
Robert H. Bloom

Start With Why
Simon Sinek
https://www.startwithwhy.com/

Growth Hacker Marketing
Ryan Holiday
http://ryanholiday.net/

The Storytelling Animal
Jonathan Gottschall
http://jonathangottschall.com/about-the-book/

Whoever Tells the Best Story Wins
Annette Simmons
http://bit.ly/14G85Ab

NOTES

Introduction

1. Andrew Stanton's quote about Mr. Rogers: http://www.ted.com/talks/andrew_stanton_the_clues_to_a_great_story/transcript?language=en

2. Jonathan Gottschall - http://jonathangottschall.com/

3. Forrester Research's Nate Elliot says Twitter and Facebook are ineffective: http://blogs.wsj.com/cmo/2014/11/17/brands-are-wasting-money-on-facebook-and-twitter-forrester-says/

Chapter 1: The keys to great storytelling

1. The average person consumes more than 100,000 words per day of content - http://hmi.ucsd.edu/howmuchinfo_research_report_consum.php

2. Chipotle Mexican Grill's "Scarecrow" video - http://bit.ly/1wqByVe

3. The Chipotle video game - www.scarecrowgame.com/game.html

4. Corey C. Delistraty in The Atlantic - www.theatlantic.com/health/archive/2014/11/the-psychological-comforts-of-storytelling/381964/

5. Dollar Shave Club video - www.youtube.com/watch?v=ZUG9qYTJMsI

6. StickerYou's World Cup story in the Toronto Star - http://bit.ly/1pw8n6m

Chapter 2: Why Steve Jobs is a Storytelling Genius

1. Jake Sorofman's five types of storytellers - blogs.gartner.com/jake-sorofman/five-types-of-brand-storytellers/

2. Steve Jobs' iPhone presentation: www.youtube.com/watch?v=c_m2F_ph_uU

3. Ron Popeil's Ronco products – www.ronco.com

Chapter 3: The time is now for startups to embrace storytelling

1. Richard Branson's decision to start Virgin Airlines after a flight to the Virgin Islands was cancelled: http://www.forbes.com/sites/johngreathouse/2013/09/03/why-richard-branson-started-virgin-airlines-the-girl-and-the-cancelled-flight/

Chapter 5: Diving into the messaging process

1. Cezary Pietrzak's Marketing Fundamentals Canvas: http://www.cezary.co/

2. "Zag" by Marty Neumeier - www.liquidagency.com/zagbook/

3. 500px – www.500px.com

4. Duke University's Ralph Keeney on the importance of having a plan for brainstorming - www.fuqua.duke.edu/news_events/news-releases/better-way-to-brainstorm/#.VLwKJy7F_Ws

5. Vigorate Digital – www.vigorate.com

Chapter 6: The messaging dividend: value propositions and more

1. Creative Common attribution for icons - www.iconfinder.com/Gimpopo

2. Peter J. Thomson's Value Proposition Canvas - www.peterjthomson.com/2013/11/value-proposition-canvas/value-proposition-canvas-example-iw

3. Adeo Ressi's MadLibs pitch format - http://fi.co/madlibs

Chapter 7: Who are the audience for your stories?

1. Field of Dreams - en.wikipedia.org/wiki/Field_of_Dreams

2. HubSpot's customer persona definition: blog.hubspot.com/marketing/buyer-persona-definition-under-100-sr

3. Buyer Persona Institute's buyer persona definition: www.buyerpersona.com/what-is-a-buyer-persona

Chapter 8: The art and science of talking to customers

1. Alex Turnbull's customer discovery exercise: www.groovehq.com/blog/customer-development

2. Freshbooks' 12-day "Roadburn" trip to meet customers - http://www.freshbooks.com/blog/tags/roadburn

Chapter 9: Creating a storytelling (marketing strategy)

1. Simon Sinek's book, "Startup With Why": www.startwithwhy.com

2. Justin Wilcos's video about "The SPA Treatment" - bit.ly/1xPC8AZ

Chapter 11: Who gets to tell stories?

1. Eric Ries' "Lean Startup": theleanstartup.com/

Chapter 12: Harness the power of influencers

1. TapInfluence's "8 Things Influencers Can Do For You" graphic: www.slideshare.net/TapInfluence/8-things-you-can-ask-influencers-to-do

2. Fred Wilson's investment in Engagio (and entrepreneur William Mougayar): http://www.businessinsider.com/engagio-founded-by-fred-wilsons-blog-commenter-thinks-you-should-manage-two-messy-inboxes-2012-2

3. Atomic Reach's Twitter chats: https://twitter.com/atomic_reach

Chapter 13 – Media Relations: setting the stage for coverage

1. 1. The Gorge's press kit: The Gorge - http://thegorge.onlinepresskit247.com/media-coverage.html

2. 2. Balsamiq's press kit - http://balsamiq.com/company/press/#presskit

3. 3. How to really earn media for your startup (Swayy) - medium.com/startup-lesson-learned/how-to-really-earn-media-for-your-startup-6a8487c78285

Chapter 14: The secrets of attracting the media spotlight

1. "Retiring at 27: Ambitious, Lazy or Crazy?": www.entrepreneur.com/article/230991

Chapter 15: Picking the time and place for PR

1. Chikodi Chima on why reporters are not algorithms: www.linkedin.com/pulse/20140807214417-1920563-public-relations-is-a-process-not-a-product-hunt

2. Robleh Jama (Tiny Hearts) – www.tinyhearts.com

Chapter 16 - How to keep the storytelling machine going

1. HubSpot's editorial calendar: offers.hubspot.com/blog-editorial-calendar

Chapter 19: An Insider's Take on Storytelling

1. Missouri University of Science and Technology eye-tracking study on how quickly people form an impression of a Website: www.sciencedaily.com/releases/2012/02/120216094726.htm

Chapter 21 - Celebrate your customers' success (aka case studies)

1. Eccolo Content Technology Content Survey Report: eccolomedia.com/eccolo-media-2014-b2b-technology-content-survey-report.pdf

Chapter 22 - Using video to pack a punch

1. Dollar Shave Club video: www.youtube.com/user/DollarShaveClub

2. Dropbox video: bit.ly/1y4sXvp

Chapter 24 - Using blogs for thought leadership and domain expertise

1. Marcus Sheridan on how to come up with 100 blog articles in 10 minutes: www.thesaleslion.com/how-to-come-up-with-100-blog-articles-for-your-business-in-10-minutes-or-less/

Chapter 26

1. The original of white papers goes back to 1922 when the U.K. government published the "The British White Paper of 1922" - http://en.wikipedia.org/wiki/Churchill_White_Paper

Chapter 27

1. Quartz surveyed 940 top-tier executives around the world to better understand how they consume news - http://insights.qz.com/ges/

2. The Moz newsletter: moz.com/moztop10

Chapter 28

1. Mojang press release after its purchase by Microsoft: mojang.com/2014/09/yes-were-being-bought-by-microsoft/

Chapter 29

1. "Startup", the podcast about the launch of a podcast network - http://gimletmedia.com/show/startup/

2. Gimlet raises $1.5-million in venture capital to create podcast network: http://blogs.wsj.com/venturecapital/2014/11/11/this-american-life-producer-raises-1-5-million-for-podcast-startup-gimlet/

ABOUT THE AUTHOR

Mark Evans is the principal with ME Consulting, which helps start-ups and fast-growing companies tell better stories (aka marketing). He has worked with dozens of startups that want strategic guidance and tactical execution to accelerate growth through a strong marketing foundation.

Before starting ME Consulting in 2008, he co-founded a startup (Blanketware) and worked for three startups (b5media, PlanetEye and Sysomos). Mark spent 15 years as an award-winning technology reporter with the National Post, Globe & Mail and Bloomberg News. He writes a popular blog about startup marketing and Canada's leading startup newsletter. Mark is a mentor with Jolt and HIGHLINE, and an advisor to The Next 36 and Venture for Canada.

When not working with startups, Mark lives in Toronto with his wife, Pamela, and three children, and strives for work/life balance by playing lots of hockey.

Mark Evans has been a professional storytelling for more than 20 years as a newspaper reporter, startup entrepreneur and marketing consultant.

"Storytelling for Startups" reflects Mark's belief that storytelling is a powerful and authentic way to engage, educate and entertain at a time when people are time-strapped, multi-tasking and overwhelmed with information.

"Storytelling for Startups" provides entrepreneurs with the ability to create their own stories (There's a storyteller in all of us!), or have the confidence and knowledge to oversee the storytelling process.

The book offers insight into the value and benefits of storytelling, puts the spotlight on good storytellers, and delivers actionable advice on how to create stories that resonate with target audiences.

Good storytelling is an essential part of Mark's business, ME Consulting, which delivers strategic counsel and tactical execution so startups and fast-growing companies can tell stories to the right people at the right time in the right places.

Mark's expertise is the development of messaging and brand positioning, strategic roadmaps, and content. You can learn more about his services and storytelling workshops at markevans.ca, and connect with Mark on Twitter via @markevans.

Manufactured by Amazon.ca
Bolton, ON